PAOLO H

FOREVER TH
SIX MONTHS Oₙ ₜₕₑ ₖₒₐ₌
WITH OASIS

PAOLO Hewitt has been for over thirty years one of the U.K.'s foremost writers on popular music. Cutting his teeth at the *NME* for seven years in the eighties, he also moonlighted as the 'Cappuccino Kid', whose musings and manifesti adorned the covers of Style Council albums.

Paolo has written over twenty books, including *Getting High: The Adventures of Oasis*, *Forever the People: Six Months on the Road with Oasis*, *Steve Marriott: All Too Beautiful* (with John Hellier), and the novel *Heaven's Promise* (all available from Dean Street Press). Other than music, recurrent themes in his writing include mod culture, football and fashion.

SELECTED TITLES BY PAOLO HEWITT

Getting High: The Adventures of Oasis
Forever the People: Six Months on the Road with Oasis
Steve Marriott: All Too Beautiful (with John Hellier)
Heaven's Promise

PAOLO HEWITT

FOREVER THE PEOPLE: SIX MONTHS ON THE ROAD WITH OASIS

With a new introduction by the author

DEAN STREET PRESS

Thanks be to that remarkable group Oasis, without whom not one word of this book would exist. Spreading out from them I would like to thank all present and correct on the Be Here Now tour, even those I never spoke to. To all the others that I made such excellent contact with, side and backstage, so many thanks.

I want to thank Johnny Chandler for examining the small print, and for his good counsel. To Clare Hulton at Boxtree for her great editorship and direction. To Sarah Jane Bacchus and Paulus plus George, Jenny and Chalfy.

Lastly, I dedicate this book to Sahika Arif, quite simply the means by which I enter the light.

Introduction to New Edition

JUST a few days before Oasis began their Be Here Now world tour, my landline phone – yes indeed! – rang. On the other end was a Mancunian, name of Noel Gallagher. 'You do know you are coming on tour with us in three days' time,' he said. 'You're the DJ.'

I didn't know I was going on tour. I had no plans to do so. But once I thought about it, the appeal started to grow. There had been pressure to follow up my Oasis biography *Getting High – The Adventures of Oasis* which had sold very well. Touring with Oasis would give me a chance to write about the band from another angle. Furthermore, acting as their DJ gave me cover. If I had gone on tour as a writer, I would have stood out. Soon as I walked into a room, people would have hushed up, stopped what they were doing or talking about. *Here's the writer* they would think and say.

As a DJ, that would not be the case. I could observe the band on the road for six months by staying in the shadows.

Why write another book about this band? Because quite simply at this time – 1997 – they were a major phenomenon. Their third album, *Be Here Now*, had sold over half a million copies – on the first day of its release.

Interest in the band was huge and did not look like going away. Oasis' fame spread itself worldwide, despite a critical reception for their third album that was built on suspect foundations. Many of the papers had lambasted its predecessor, *(What's The Story) Morning Glory?*, only to see it sell eleven million copies. They were not going to make that mistake again. *Be Here Now*'s deficiencies were glossed over and reviews all tilted to the positive. Yet some were not enamoured by the work, even within the Oasis camp.

Released in August, by December the album's creator Noel Gallagher had started to express his disdain for the work.

People join bands for many reasons. Money, fame, sex are three usual motivators. But another is to escape routine, jobs, the nine to five. On this tour, Oasis discovered that being one of the biggest bands in the world meant different demands being placed upon them, that the routine designed to avoid the nine to five simply became a routine of five to nine instead.

As one commentator put it, Oasis were great at wanting to be the biggest band in the world but actually playing that role was completely different.

Oasis, at this point, still epitomised rock'n'roll bad boy behaviour. Liam refusing to go on tour, Liam being arrested for cocaine possession at seven in the morning, Noel telling the nation that he put cocaine on his cornflakes every morning: these were just a few of their favourite things. Now, such behaviour had to be curtailed. Crowds of thirty, forty thousand or more had paid good money. This was the big time. That which had helped make them famous had to be put aside. Simply because the financial stakes were too high.

When Liam stormed off stage during a gig in New Zealand, he told all who would listen that as far as he was concerned Oasis were finished. The next day, after a meeting with the band's manager, in which the huge cost of cancelling the impending South American tour was laid out to the singer, Oasis were put back into action.

Other notable differences: the band now had a stage show – of sorts. At every gig they would appear from a telephone box. Halfway through, Noel would take a solo spot, opening up with a ballad-paced version of the John Lennon song 'Help' and then playing his own songs. Two keyboard players had been added to the line-up. After the gig, chauffeur-driven cars whisked each band member separately back to the hotel. The days of the band travelling as one on a coach were over.

The personnel employed to make the Be Here Now tour happen numbered fifty-four people.

When they did gather together as a band in these new circumstances, talk would inevitably drift back to simpler times, days when they were stuffed into a tiny van, hitting the road, playing every gig offered, even if it meant just two people in the audience. The rise to the top is always more enjoyable than the stay at the summit.

The template for *Forever The People* was 1963's *Love Me Do – The Beatles Progress*, written by Michael Braun. This ranks as one of the best Beatles books because of its unflinching and intimate look at the Fabs. I was much taken by it and I hope I got somewhere near its power in this work.

Paolo Hewitt
London 2020

THE PROLOGUE

FIRST time ever I spoke to him was late Thursday night on 18 August 1994. It was at an after-show party for Oasis, held at the Leisure Lounge, Holborn, in London. The band had just played the Astoria Theatre.

I forget who made the introduction but it was a brief chat. Nothing special, nothing memorable, nothing to suggest that I would later write two books about him and his band, his music.

I did so because, like so many people in this country, I believe Oasis are one of the bands of the decade. My belief in them began the night a good friend played me the demo of 'Live Forever'. It was a triumphant moment – one I will not forget. The song activated that tingle inside, the magic shiver that occurs to us all when we hear something special. Truly special. Suffice to say that the more I heard, the more I saw, the more I flipped. I was not alone. Oasis smashed into our lives and they were intoxicating.

Like all great bands, their timing was spot on. All bands that aspire to greatness have to catch the *Zeitgeist* and Oasis did it magnificently. Thank God they did, for if, like me, you slept through most of the appalling '80s, then you'll know why Oasis were the wake-up call of the decade. Their music made you want to holler, their records, like all the great ones, inspired and thrilled you. Especially if you came from a similar part of town to them. Oasis said take no shit and face the fuckers full on. Armed with their tunes, that's exactly what you did.

They brought back rock music, made it relevant again. To be honest, I hadn't really bothered with the stuff for years but Oasis turned me round. They came along and emphasized its power through their music, its glamour through their errant behaviour.

They made me want to hear not only their records but a thousand others. Heady stuff but it was simple. Oasis, like so many of their peers, grew up hating the '80s (until Acid House came along) and so they went back further – primarily to the '60s but with these boys the '70s as well – to draw their inspiration from.

Noel Gallagher took the musical classicism of those decades, added some modern music – I'm thinking of hip hop and House and artists such as Beck – and then twisted it all into his own thing. He ripped off millions of artists but that didn't matter because when he stole riffs or melodies he either covered it up brilliantly or he made them entirely his own. As another musician once said, he takes the most obvious chords there are but makes them sound like you have never heard them before. That's some talent.

The Oasis sound – Noel's aural vision realized – was huge, primal, classic, electrifying and glorious. At the centre of this thrilling storm was Liam's unique vocal, an unholy mix of Lennon and Rotten that was delivered with a very real passion and swagger. (I once called him a soul singer and he reared back in defiance, shouting, 'I'm rock'n'roll, mate.')

The result was a series of great singles and the emergence of a talented band who made no bones about what they wanted. And what they wanted was good old-fashioned rock stardom, the kind punk – which inspired them in the first place – sought to destroy.

This would be the first of many contradictions, because Oasis wanted it all. They wanted big houses, big wardrobes, big cars, loads of money and all the trimmings on top, please. In keeping with the temper of the '90s, they were men who declined to hide their desires. They stated everything clearly. We do this, we want that. And the fuckers got it big time. But what it did to them is yet to be revealed.

*

Thinking about it now, I have to say that I actually liked Noel a hell of a lot before I actually met him. That's because in interviews he would say things like, 'I know we're going to be ripped off like all the other bands but as long as my name goes down with Lennon and McCartney, Pete Townshend, Marriott and Lane, when we finish, I don't give a shit.'

So when I was introduced to Noel that night at the Leisure Lounge, I chose not to tell him that we had already crossed paths at that year's Glastonbury. On that occasion he was so gone, so fucked up on alcohol and chemicals, that I doubt he would have remembered me anyway. The man literally couldn't talk. He just stood there, gazing. Then he walked.

That was Saturday night. Sunday afternoon, Oasis played and I can still remember that ripple of excitement which shot through that vast crowd when they appeared, a real acknowledgement that something special was being unveiled on that roily grey day. And so it proved.

Obviously I would see them play far far better gigs but at that point Oasis were on such a roll you could just feel it in the wet air. Afterwards myself and a friend went backstage. He was E'd up and desperately wanted to meet Noel, who he had spied slumped against the bar. I'm no good in such situations, so I stayed put while my mate rushed over to him.

When he came back he said the conversation had gone something like this:

'Fucking great gig, mate.'

No reply from Noel. Not a flicker.

'Your band are really fucking special.'

Again, no reply.

'My E kicked in when you went into "Live Forever".'

That was more like it.

'Fucking top one, mate,' Noel Gallagher firmly replied.

And then he looked up, his craggy face distorted by a huge smile, the satisfaction of a job well done smeared large in his eyes.

Noel knew of me anyway. He'd read my work in the music press, enjoyed my book on The Jam. And then we started to bump into each other intermittently. Once at an Ocean Colour Scene gig at the Water Rats where a girl I was with asked him outright what he did and was it enjoyable?

He just smiled and then anxiously looked at me to see if this was a wind-up. I didn't blame him. His first album had just shot into the charts at number one and Noel's face was painted all over town. I nodded apologetically, shrugged my shoulders, mouthed the word 'girls!'.

In those days there was something of a clumsiness between myself and Noel. It wasn't so much a major sussing-out operation, just shyness on both our parts. After seeing them at places like Brighton round about Christmas '95 (The La's offering surreal support) I'd come up with inane lines to Noel like, 'Great gig, you really pulled it off tonight' and he would reply, 'Yeah, cheers.'

Then silence. He gave no space for further talk and I didn't know how to create any.

January then came and one night Noel unexpectedly called up, invited me over to the flat he was renting off Johnny Marr. Meg Matthews, who had just started seeing Noel at the time, opened the door. I was impressed. The sitting room was absolutely enormous.

Noel was sat in front of a TV watching the interview he and Liam had undertaken with Gary Crowley for Carlton TV's now defunct *Beat* show. I would soon learn that watching himself on the small screen was and still is one of Noel's favourite hobbies.

Many times, as he fixed on the screen, his body language demanding silence, it was as if he was carefully observing not himself but some other fascinating creature. That's how intent his gaze was. It was obvious too, as he unravelled his background through many entertaining anecdotes, that he was something of an outsider. Noel's parents were Irish, he grew up in Manchester and now he was in London, a town that draws real suspicion and derision from some Northern folk.

As I would discover, Noel transcended such low levels of thought. He knew more than anyone that parochialism is the enemy of ambition. He wouldn't let anything get in the way of the bigger picture. He was the first band member to move down here. He was fiercely proud of Manchester, its customs, the majority of the people, but he felt stifled. So he had to leave, had to breathe, had to make it.

At our first get-together Noel told me that in his first six London weeks he barely knew a soul. He lived in a tiny flat in Chiswick and he took taxis everywhere because he couldn't for the life of him work out the Underground system. The map of tube lines was a meaningless plate of coloured spaghetti to Noel Gallagher.

That night we drank a lot, talked some. Then other people arrived, a party started happening. I got out at about four that morning and woke with a bad hangover but a good memory.

Not long after, Noel moved to Camden, took a flat not far from where I lived. Now I would visit more regularly, arriving early evening, leaving as dawn was breaking. We more often than not got blitzed and I reeled in amazement at his stamina. It was and still is enormous.

After some parties I would crawl off home in the early hours and when I'd return the next day he would still be drinking, still at it.

'You've kept going?' I'd say in amazement. He'd turn slowly to me with that lazy, triumphant look on his face.

'No surrender,' he'd say, 'no surrender.'

We talked more, delved further into our backgrounds. We discovered several things in common, which is in no way strange. All music writers find similarities with musicians whose work they admire because it is those experiences that inform the music they are attracted to in the first place.

In the case of Noel and I, it was, to mention a few, unholy childhoods, working-class life, football, politics, UFOs, music, the same sense of humour, Catholicism, films and the same passion for dousing our brains in whatever so we could loosen up, let out secrets, ideas or hidden stories about ourselves.

In comparison with Johnny Marr's Fulham abode, Noel's flat was tiny, compact. He stayed here quite a long time and it was weird because soon his fame would grow to be a billion times bigger than his home. The place was never messy but he didn't seem to keep much there in the way of records, clothes or books. The Beatles were a constant presence in the form of pictures he had placed on the wall but there was just as much Oasis memorabilia. I have to say Noel was not only great company – always witty, humorous and interesting – but right from the off he was a fascinating subject.

He would always blow up everything he did into a drama, as if he felt life was so damn straight and dull and boring that he had to bend it into exciting shapes so as to grab and entertain you. As another friend once remarked, 'You have to put a 20 per cent commission on all he says.'

Even a one-minute walk to the shop for cigs always had some incident or snatch of dialogue worth playing back. Suffice to say, that if they ever invent an after-dinner speaking circuit for ex-rock stars, Noel Gallagher, without a shadow of doubt, will be its highest earner. Superb timing, good eye for detail, inordinate reservoirs of charm and a million anecdotes – the boy will clean up.

During those heady evenings I noticed too his growing need to be the centre of attention. At first he granted you equal billing, but as time wore on he began to place himself first. It accounted a lot, I believed, for his factitious relationship with Liam, who also and very eagerly craves the spotlight, the attention. Noel was the perfect host but you always knew who was at the centre of the night's gravity. That was party time, the midnight hours of abandonment filled with a million words and laughs.

Sober or alone in the cold light of day, that was another story. More often than not, this is when Noel retreated into his shell. And when it became hardest to break him into conversation, to hear him enthusiastically seize upon an idea – like he did the night before – and improvise on it like the riffs he conjures up so effortlessly on his guitar.

Of course, part of this reticence was to do with a mighty hangover. But much of it was down to Noel's very real need for privacy, for secrecy. Which he made no secret of. In so many of his songs he tells his subject that he can't commit fully, that he/she will never see the full man.

And if, in an effort to break that silence, you pushed too hard, Noel would assume his bad-head look, the one that firmly said, my friend, tread very, very carefully.

Other times, in unguarded moments, he would display a real vulnerability, where you were allowed to glimpse snatches of weakness. It is why Meg's girlfriends fussed around him, he had that little-boy-lost look down pat. Which was all quite at odds with the cheerful, entertaining loud-mouth you found in that day's paper making bold and provocative pronouncements.

I mentioned this duality to Meg once and she explained it to me, said that Noel was a Gemini, double personality. Maybe. Or maybe it's because duality is a requisite of the songwriter's nature. Musicians must bear contradictory natures. If they don't, it's a major contradiction.

Noel – and rightfully so – wants respect for his song-writing talent. He has an urge to be taken seriously, to be viewed as an artist. But unlike many others with similar temperaments he also wants the clichés of rock-star life, the trappings of cars, designer goods, the huge properties.

He will talk loud about his talent but be affected by a review in the music press by someone who obviously don't know shit. He would voraciously devour music biographies but keep his reading habits a secret.

He has a lively intelligence that he chooses sometimes to mask with uncomfortable sullenness. You can spend hours of closeness with him but then he won't call you for days on end.

He would unveil great theories on music. He'd tell you that Paul McCartney invented punk rock. Uh? Because Macca wrote 'Helter Skelter', the song that inspired The Stooges, who in turn begat the Pistols.

And then – as you'll later see – he would follow that up with some divvy statement like America has only ever produced two bands of worth, The Stooges and The MC5. The rest are all absolute rubbish. Sometimes, he spouted such nonsense as a wind-up. Noel loves to argue, to get you at it. But mostly he was serious when it came to discussing music. Watch out as well, for he never admits defeat. Even if you disprove his argument a hundred times, he'll come back every time. Noel Gallagher is one stubborn kind of fellow.

Musically, he adored the Pistols (their debut is the finest piece of rock'n'roll music ever) and the early Who and The Jam and The Smiths and The Stone Roses.

He loved writing but he cursed it as well, for it exhausted him and brought to the surface all kinds of unwelcome moods and feelings. (I often said his songs were his real bank balance. As long as there was 30 in the account he was fine. He could relax. A little.)

Noel was fiercely disciplined about his writing and his work. He'd party 24 hours but come showtime he'd be ready and able and standing by his station, guns at the ready. He fretted big time over his lyrics, especially when Oasis went into popularity overdrive and he was severed from his council-estate roots. Suddenly, writing about his life became untenable. It was far too unreal. Who else could relate unless it was one of his real musician mates such as Johnny Marr? He now had to work so much harder to dig up the broken jewels inside.

*

Cinema and comedy were two other passions. And it wasn't just one type of comedy either. His tastes ranged from the sophisticated – *Seinfeld*, *Larry Sanders* – to the crass – the film *Dumb and Dumber*. He adored Bill Hicks, Peter Cook, Dudley Moore, Billy Connolly and he loved *The Fast Show*. With a mighty passion.

Knowing his background, it was good to see Noel laugh. More than anyone I knew, Noel seemed to have transcended his brutal childhood, to have left all the violence and the terror behind as he forged spectacularly ahead both in his career and as a person. People with similar backgrounds wondered at how the scars never showed. Noel rarely referred to his family life past but he leaned heavily on the women closest to him, mother Peggy and wife Meg.

He often said that he would never write a song about his fractured childhood because it was nobody's business but his own. I agreed but I also suspected a cover-up. I think that one day he will confront his demons armed only with his guitar just as one day he may well write a song with the words 'I love you' in it.

I grew to like the man immensely. I think if you ask anyone who has spent time with him they'll say the same thing. And being a writer, pretty soon I wanted to create *the* book. I felt I was in a great position to catch his actions and words, allow myself and others to gain an understanding of his talent and the whole Oasis phenomenon.

Then I got lucky.

Noel asked me to DJ for Oasis at some of their gigs. It was a good shout. It allowed me to observe them on the road but not have the burden of being known as the writer, in which case they may well have tempered their behaviour or clammed up. (Then again, probably not.)

Starting with a warm-up gig in Southend and ending at Knebworth, it was amazing to see this band fly, to see them effortlessly place themselves firmly into the centre of Britain's musical and cultural life, to witness inside and outside this country, their ascent into levels of popularity that hadn't been since the Fab Four.

I loved them because they achieved all this with righteous songs that were fuck all to do with frivolity and everything to do with class and quality. It was a massive achievement.

Obviously I got to know the other band members. They were everything I thought they would be. Respectful but totally suspicious at first (as were the whole road crew for at least a year, which was right) piss-takers, funny as fuck, absolutely loyal to themselves and this thing called Oasis, temperamental, down to earth, witty, wise, hedonistic and absolutely loyal to each other, to the gang.

Liam kept his distance for the longest. I think the fame thing did his head in at first and he was secretly trying to find his feet, work out what, who was real, who wasn't. Still, he attracted a lot of people to him, which wasn't surprising. Where Noel was quiet, Liam was loud. He was also funny, a great dresser and very knowledgeable. Especially about music. He knew his tunes, Liam, and he was also sharp enough to exploit the press image of him as a simple lout. Liam laid it on thick for most interviewers because he knew what made a good story. Plus he was fighting Noel for the column inches. Guigsy and Bonehead acted as a kind of buffer zone for Noel and Liam. I once wrote about the first time I saw Oasis, how the brothers acted onstage as if they were daring anyone to take them on physically. What I forgot to add was that Guigsy and Bonehead also played with expressions that said, Yeah, and if you get past them you've got us to deal with now.

Offstage they were far more relaxed, Guigsy lighting huge spliffs and kicking off football arguments, Bonehead filling his throat with wine and looking for some mad escapade to keep him amused. I never met their first drummer, Tony McCarroll (although I certainly heard about him), but I already knew Alan White before he joined the group through his older brother, Steve. Whitey had the same glint in his eye as Bonehead, that look which made you think they were up to something. Even when they weren't. Which was rare. On the Be Here Now tour, it was no surprise that those two became firm friends.

As their success increased at an unbelievable speed so my life took strange, exciting turns. I would find myself sitting alone with Noel in his dressing room after he had just played Earls Court the first time. And outside, as he wiped away the last drop of sweat, you could still hear the crowd baying for more.

I remember the very night when Noel and Liam argued like fuck and then Noel casually unveiled his song 'The Masterplan' in the studio and the music took my breath away. (It was why I dedicated the first chapter of my book to that whole experience.) I recall too finding myself in Cannes with Noel and him saying to the actor Dennis Hopper, 'Hi, my name's Noel, I'm in Oasis' and Hopper replying, 'Oasis? What the fuck is that?'

In dreams I still touch the growing excitement of that amazing Knebworth weekend, culminating on Sunday night with fireworks in the skies and fireworks in our heads. I remember a lot of laughter, I remember a lot of arguing. I remember that period as one in which I seemed to greet the dawn more and more and see less and less of the day. It was all good.

Knebworth was the end of Oasis phase one. Two things now occurred. One, the tabloids made them a priority.

Two, Oasis had no idea what to do next. Really, in the perfect world, they should have knocked it on the head.

Instead they took a break. Funny things happened. We went to see Weller support Gabrielle at Ronnie Scott's. Afterwards we went looking for cabs. We got one. But there were too many of us. So Noel asked a passing dustbin driver and his mates for a lift to St John's Wood. And that's how he arrived in that exclusive part of town, singing songs with the dustmen.

Noel went away to Mustique and wrote and demoed the next album. He came back and they rehearsed for an MTV special. On the final day Liam bailed out. Noel hit him and then had to do the show on his own. Naturally, with his brother watching, he pulled it off superbly. One-nil.

He sang (not very well, due to nerves) with Burt Bacharach and then they rehearsed for America. It was too much too soon. Liam stood them up at the airport and went home. Front-page news. One-all.

Clever sod that he is, Noel said to Marcus, tell Liam he isn't needed over here anyway. It worked. Liam was on the first plane out to America. He shouldn't have bothered. Within a week it had gone pear-shaped again.

Liam continued playing the brat and Noel finally blew up in North Carolina, cancelled the tour and came home alone. It was the only time I worried about him. He looked dazed and lost walking through that airport. Still, he was front page news. Two-one.

During this time it was hard to get hold of Noel. No more quick calls and bombing round for a session. He'd moved now to St John's Wood while his million-pound house, Supernova Heights in Belsize Park, was readied for living in. He rarely returned phone calls, preferring to get Meg or his office to make the move.

Now when you went to visit him there would be fans outside the house or journalists scrutinizing you. Now when the doorbell rang at five in the morning it wasn't refreshments arriving, it was a reporter desperate for a quote. The constant requests pissed Noel off but he loved it as well.

I told him of a Malcolm Muggeridge observation on success. You go out one day and you get pestered and you think, why the fuck can't everyone just leave me alone? The next day your wish is granted. Now you're worried. No-one is saying a word. What's going on? Am I still popular? Am I still loved? Can I make a living? You can't win.

I now think a little piece of Noel was lost in this frenzied time because suddenly it wasn't fun any more. Now he was on a roller-coaster and no one knew the destination. He was now a major public figure whose every action was scrutinized. He had vast wealth and a million ways to deal with it. He had people relying on him for their living.

I can't see how anyone couldn't be affected. Noel certainly was because he had to sacrifice spontaneity to keep this whole strange operation on the rails. Sometimes he only seemed happy when onstage or writing or surrounded by the trusted few. I can't speak for others but I know I got affected in some way by this relentless spotlight. I'd never known anyone so fucking famous and suddenly I wasn't so quick to take the piss, not so quick to criticize, for fear of upsetting an already uptight situation that had been exasperated further by the prying world outside.

Yet despite it all Noel had his humour by his side. Many a time he used it to puncture himself. I just think that fame put a shield around him and I was not up to breaking it enough times. And some days I think that's what he really wanted, maybe needed. They decided to start recording as soon as possible after the American debacle. It was crucial they show unity. They went into Abbey Road studios. It was announced that Liam and Patsy were going to get married but in secret. Front-page news everywhere. Two-all.

Noel wasn't having that. So he announced that he and Meg were also due to tie the knot in the same week. Front-page news everywhere. Three-two. Liam went mad, hurled an ashtray through a studio window. Then he got warned for allegedly retaliating against some cyclist in Camden Town and then arrested for possession of cocaine. But everyone knew it would be sorted. Who would jail such a popular figure, the nation's fave?

The band left Abbey Road, retreated into a residential studio in the country. Too many stories were being leaked to the press. It was someone within, someone close. I worried occasionally that the finger pointed at me. I worried about the people behind my back slagging me off to Noel.

And ultimately I realized – despite my outer protestations – that a friendship with someone so famous could never be as normal as the ones I have with other people. It would always be a different beast.

Noel put everything into the making of the next album. It came to dominate him. If we went to a gig (another one of his favourite activities) he would always chop just before the end, go back to the studio, that distant look in his eyes. He never invited me there as the sessions got underway.

As the weeks passed, you'd say, 'How's the album going?' and he'd give a one-word answer: 'Good.' He didn't encourage you to ask any more. So you didn't. You left him to deal with the pressure alone.

I went to the residential studio, once. I heard 'Fade In/Out' and 'My Sister Lover' and I think 'Stand By Me'. I was overwhelmed at how large the music had gotten. It was Noel saying success has not softened me.

They moved back to London for the last leg and then I would visit the studios more regularly. Mark Coyle was always there. He's an old friend of Noel's, maybe the closest to him. Mark is a musician, knows the life. He knew that Noel was pulling out all the stops.

With Owen Morris in tow they fashioned a dense-sounding album because Noel couldn't leave it alone. He had too much money to draw upon and a growing ego which demanded more from him each week.

Of course, *Be Here Now* didn't work for anyone. It didn't work for Creation because they foolishly announced that it would outsell *Morning Glory*. It didn't work for Oasis because it failed to live up to many of their crowd's high expectations and it didn't work for Noel because it placed his talent in doubt.

His cause wasn't helped when he socialized publicly with Tony Blair. Or when he dreamt up the visuals around the album that said nothing more than Oasis are just rich hooligans. All of us knew they were so much more than that.

By now Noel had renegotiated his publishing deal. He bought another house, a retreat located in real splendour and beautiful country, a place where a million trees surround his house.

The parties got bigger. There was more space to fill. More people entered his life. Some stayed, others fell away. Then he called me up one day and said, 'You know you're coming on tour with us on Sunday.'

And that was it. No please or thank you. Just six months on the road with Oasis. With Noel. With the band. Where there would be changes and new situations, experiences and stories.

This book then is my version of those six months, September '97 to March '98. It is my truth, my reality. It may correspond with the band's version or that of the 56-strong crew that travelled the world with them. It may not. Whatever. I'm just lucky to have all these memories, to be on the roller-coaster.

Paolo Hewitt, March 1999

ONE

IT'S THAT TIME OF THE MOUTH AGAIN

The United Kingdom

True or false?

Ars est celare artem (Art lies in concealing the art).

Weird. So weird.

In public, you often saw him jumping out of large, dark-coloured cars, waving to crowds, flicking V signs, burly drivers rushing to protect him as the cameras fire off in all directions and the air is filled with shouts of 'Noel! Noel! Look over here, Noel.'

Today was different. Today he – one of the nation's most familiar faces – strolled totally unnoticed across the concourse of Paddington Station, his wife Meg by his side. He was dressed in a black corduroy suit, a white polo-neck shirt, and he wore sunglasses which covered half his face.

He spotted me watching him as I nursed a cappuccino and he came straight over and demanded, 'Did you ring me up at two this morning?'

Probably not but could well have done. The night before I had got lost in myself. What occurred at my house in the early hours of the morning was anyone's guess.

'Not sure, Noel.'

'Just about to go to kip and the phone rang but when I finally got to it there was no one there. Thought it's got to be you, you dick.'

'Thanks.'

He looked around at the busy platform, the passengers swarming around like flies. 'What train we on? What platform is it?' he asked.

'Fuck knows.'

'Oh, you're going to be a lot of good on this tour, you are, a fat lot of fucking good.'

*

To tour: to enter a bubble where the real world has no meaning, to frazzle mind, to exhaust body. To escape routine only to crave it back with a vengeance.

On tour: the only place in the world where one minute you want to tell someone your darkest secret and the next day you want to badly hurt them. With tongue, with fists. Where room numbers are a blur and the bar is your sitting room. Where promises are made and sometimes even kept.

Another Oasis tour, six months around the world. Why? To sell records, to keep the band's profile alive, but above all to keep the group buoyant, interested.

'When the album was finished I deliberately didn't mention the touring word because of all the strain that it has put on the band in the past,' Marcus Russell, their manager, revealed. 'I thought let them come to me and sure enough, about a month later they started saying things like, "Well, what's happening with the gigs?"'

No surprise there. Oasis like to tour. They enjoy the life, the work. They like waking up in strange places with strange hangovers. They like being able to cause chaos simply by walking out of an airport. And they like, above all, having their work validated by vast audiences because, like all performers, applause, attention are essential to their well-being. Applause is magical. It washes away all doubts.

Oasis needed that applause right now. For the first time in their history – and they knew this too – they no longer looked or felt invincible. 'D'You Know What I Mean?' the lead-off single from *Be Here Now*, had only stayed number one for a week. It gave unwelcome ammunition to their growing chorus of critics. A strange feeling for the band, this one, almost shocking.

They'd never encountered it before. Success was their natural birthright.

Now it was playing hard to get. And Oasis were on the defensive.

Their problem could be stated simply. In late 1997 this was a band in search of meaning. They had risen so swiftly, so dramatically, they now faced the question that no band has yet successfully answered. How do you maintain that rush of excitement which accompanies every new band's rise to the top? How do you keep that momentum going? And while you're at it, where exactly do you perform after you've played the biggest-ever UK gigs? This six-month tour would give them the answers. But not the ones they expected.

*

The first time I heard the finished version of *Be Here Now* was in the Air Studios, Hampstead. It was Saturday 20 February 1997. The album, bar a few tweaks and dubs, was finished. Time now for the playback. I arrived at about ten that night and, naturally, Liam and Noel were bickering.

'Come on, I'm mad for hearing these tunes,' Liam complained, restlessly wandering around the studio. He was dressed in a dark, bulky jacket, half length. Noel had on jeans and a plain T-shirt. They were both clean-shaven. 'All right,' Noel testily replied, ever the perfectionist.

'They'll be ready in a minute.' He shivered in annoyance at his brother's impatience.

'What's the fucking wait?' the singer demanded.

'Just a few more minutes, all right?' the songwriter barked back. Noel then turned to producer Owen Morris and whispered something about overdubs. Liam sat down huffily, about ten feet behind his brother.

'Right,' Noel finally said. 'Put down the lights.'

'About fucking time,' the singer said.

Noel shot him a withering look. Liam stared back at him. Challenging.

Also present in the room were Meg, Liam's wife Patsy Kensit, plus Mark Coyle and Phil Smith, who have known and worked with Oasis over the years. All of them were quiet, expectant. This music had taken seven months to realize.

Feedback, guitars, bass, drums, sonic effect now filled the huge speakers. The drinks on the table started to shake. Suddenly the musical dust settled and the band strode magnificently into 'Do You Know What I Mean?'.

As his voice filled the studio, attacked us from all angles, Liam walked forward to stand by his brother and listen hard. Noel turned and smiled. Then he put his arm around his younger brother and the pair of them spontaneously started dancing and laughing at this thing they had achieved.

*

After the release of *Be Here Now* (an event that reached such a fever pitch in the media that Noel skipped the country for a few days), Oasis discovered themselves under fire from many directions. This in itself wasn't new. They had now learnt that success is impossible without hatred. What caught them on the hop was the growing feeling that we had seen it all before.

New album? Sounds like the old one. Public image? Boring. Seen it, spat at it, done it. Noel and Liam? Arrogant/overbearing.

Unthinkable. Where once their miscreant public behaviour excited people, now they just came over as petulant. Oasis were being charged with the sin of boredom and there was nothing they could do about it. Time and success had robbed them of their newness, their freshness. There was nothing left for people to discover about them.

To add to their problems, some new kids appeared, looking to make it big and, irony of irony, they were real close friends of the band. Throughout 1997 the sight of the pendulum shifting towards The Verve was unmistakable. Their single 'Bitter Sweet Symphony' became the year's 'Wonderwall'. Ditto *Urban Hymns* for *Morning Glory*. They were the band that now got people excited, made people want to get close and know more about them.

Of course, it wasn't all dark. Oasis remained hugely popular. Two out of three of the singles taken from the album would effortlessly enter the charts at number one. The album sold in the millions. In fact, one of the tour's most repeated phrases occurred when *Be Here Now* was mentioned. 'Oh,' either band or management would smugly say, 'you mean *that* failure of an LP which has only sold eight million copies worldwide?'

That was certainly Noel's take, his self-defence mechanism against those who would bring him down, who would remind him that the frisson which once surrounded Oasis had now evaporated.

One night he told me, 'I said to Marcus how much has the album sold and he said, "Well, it's not looking too good. We've only sold six million copies so far." Six million copies! I've sold six million albums. Fucking hell, you dick, I was on the dole five years ago.'

But there was a definite perception that the band were fighting, a feeling that Oasis had lost something, had sacrificed some of their wilder instincts along the road. Noel took drinks with the Prime Minister and the symbolism of Noel relaxed in Number Ten, the heart of the Establishment, convinced people that he had swapped his rebel soul for ego, for transitory fame.

So on this tour, to regain lost ground, the band would have to prove themselves all over again, show that they hadn't lost it. And this is what they had discovered. That in the end a band's life boiled down to proving yourself again and again and again. And even then that might not be enough.

*

Oasis began their 'Be Here Now Live' tour in August by rehearsing in South London's Music Bank and then shifting for the final week of rehearsals to the London Arena in Docklands. I watched the final day of the band's preparation but it told me little because Liam had a throat infection and didn't show up on stage.

In the car on the way home Noel said, 'Guess where our album went in the States?'

'One?'

'No, two. Guess what's one? Puff Daddy.'

This was the artist that had knocked 'D'You Know What I Mean?' off the top slot after only a week, giving rise to the notion that Oasis's popularity was swiftly falling.

Referring to a recent headline (in which he had asserted the band's popularity over religion), Noel settled back in his seat and said, 'Puff Daddy is bigger than God. It's official.'

*

A mate of mine and me – this is true – we nearly scrapped over the Oasis album. 'It's shit,' he said. 'You only like it because you have to.'

'I like it. I like that album. Not because I know them but because I like it. All right?'

And for a minute it looked like it might go off between us.

But I did. Like the album. Not because I was close – and this is genuine – but because I rate it, still do all these months down the line. If it were my baby I would have dropped two songs, 'I Hope, I Think, I Know' and 'Me And My Big Mouth', and re-recorded 'It's Getting Better, Man,' as a full-on Northern Soul song – which is what it primarily is. (Imagine the guitars as horns.)

The rest of the material I would happily live with because – and I'll argue it with anyone – there is still much to admire. The title track, 'D'You Know What I Mean?', 'Stand By Me,' 'Fade In/Out', 'All Around The World', 'Magic Pie', 'Don't Go Away', even 'The Girl With The Dirty Shirt' – these are fine songs, a wide cross-section of music.

I like the size of this album, its intent to overwhelm. I like the way Noel tried to shift his songwriting style, to expand upon the structures of the songs, and approach verse and chorus differently.

Furthermore, I couldn't understand how Oasis could be written off so swiftly. It said much about the speed we now live our lives at. Oasis is number one for a week? Jesus, haven't you heard one is all, everywhere else is nowhere. And second? Second means jack shit.

*

As a warm-up for the UK tour, Oasis played three dates in Scandinavia. The Spektrum in Oslo hosted the first show. Ocean Colour Scene played support and all 9600 tickets had been sold.

At the soundcheck, Noel and Liam stood by the mixing desk surveying the stage. This was filled with replicas from the *Be Here Now* album cover. There was a fake bar under which two session musicians, Mike Rowe and Paul Stacey, would sit and supplement the Oasis sound with their keyboards and samples. There was a phone box through which the band would make their entrance every night. And there was Alan White's drum kit placed above a replica of the front of a Rolls-Royce, thus elevating him a few feet above the band. The brothers stood admiring the handiwork and then Liam said, 'I'm mad for doing a gig.'

He was all hunched up in his dark parka, white fur flicking through his longish hair. Noel nodded eagerly in agreement. 'Me as well,' he replied. 'In fact, I'm so mad for it I think I'll explode when I get onstage. Just blow up everywhere. Or just blow my head up. One of the fucking two.' Liam laughed but he slyly gave his elder brother a look. Fuck me, he was saying, even I don't know where you're coming from sometimes.

*

Half an hour later Liam said, 'Everyone, right, goes on about how mad I am but what about that cunt? Normal, sensible Noel. Mr Straight, Mr Misery. Fuck that. Do you know what he did the other day? We were all sitting in the control room and he comes in, looks around, sniffs the air and says, "It smells of balloons in here." Smells of balloons! How weird is that?'

*

The night before the Oslo gig the band went to a bar opposite the hotel. It was Sunday 7 September 1997 and the talk soon came round to previous Scandinavian missions. Noel, as ever, was first off.

'Do you remember that gig where I got so out of it that I passed out and you cunts left me behind at the gig? I woke up and I had no idea where I was, where the hotel was or how I was going to get there. Every fucker's gone. They're just about to lock up the building. So I wander outside and this guy comes up on a scooter. "Ah, Noel Gallagher, I take you home." So we drive to every hotel in town until we find the right one. Turns out this guy is part of some Chilean resistance movement and he's living here in exile. How weird is that being rescued by a Chilean freedom fighter in the middle of nowhere. Top, it was.'

'I don't remember that,' Bonehead said, a slight frown on his face. 'Where was I?'

'The last time I saw you,' Noel said, 'you were holding two hot dogs and threatening to beat up some guy.'

'Oh, yeah,' Bonehead said, brightening up and then finishing off his beer with a big gulp. "Cos I was.'

*

The next day Noel holds a press conference. 'Would you play for the Pope?' is one question.

'No, never.'

'But if you did, what would you play?'

Noel considers his answer.

'"Some Might Pray",' he offers. With a smirk.

*

In the dressing room, Liam said to an over-eager Scandinavian fan, 'Get away, you're smothercating me.' Then he paused and turned to Bonehead. 'Is that a word. "Smothercate"?'

Bonehead looked up.

'It's the Irish for Mothercare.'

*

Onstage, during an unremarkable gig (they would only hot up on the third date in Copenhagen), Liam dedicated 'Live Forever' to Princess Diana. Noel shot him a withering look. Not as bad as the one he gave him that Friday night at Glastonbury when Liam motioned for Robbie Williams to join them onstage. But a bad one all the same.

Afterwards Liam stood in a long corridor with sweat stains visible on his T-shirt. Noel passed by and noticed them. 'What's that? Sweating out all the gear?'

'Nah, man, sweating out my soul.'

*

The next day one paper's headline read: 'Liam – No drink! No drugs!' They were referring to an ear infection he had picked up the week before, medication for which prevented his usual indulgences. 'The fuckers,' Liam exclaimed. 'If I get drunk they have a go. If I'm sober they have a go. They ain't going to be happy until I'm six feet under.' Then he jabbed his finger at the photo of him singing onstage and shouted, 'Come on!' But he did so as if he was shouting at someone he didn't know at all. But greatly and truly admired.

*

Two dates followed. The Globen in Stockholm and The Forum in Copenhagen. After the first show the band briefly attended a party in their honour. But the club was packed and they had boxed the band off in a special area with a rope and security all around them so there seemed no room for fun or antics. They quickly split. After the next show Oasis crowded the hotel bar and mixed in with old flames Ocean Colour Scene. Voices were raised, drinks spilt.

The next day, with hangovers, Oasis gathered at the airport for the flight to London and the start of the UK tour. Noel and I went for food and Liam too thought that a good idea. We sat eating in silence until Noel looked up from his plate and said to me, "The studio has been put in at Supernova Heights now.'

Before I could answer, Liam butted in. 'Well, when are we going to do something?' he demanded, his belligerent voice carrying far. 'Mad to make some music, me. When are you going to invite me over? Come on, when?'

'Pretty soon,' Noel nonchalantly replied.

'Pretty soon? You've been living there years now and I still haven't seen the gaff. Every other fucker has,' he complained. Noel shrugged his shoulders as if saying, 'So what?' The house was obviously his sanctuary from all Oasis-related matters. Including, that would seem, his brother.

Liam changed tack, calmed his voice down. 'Look, if we put something together, you can take the credit, you can have the money, I'm arsed about that. Just mad to make music, me.'

Again, no reply. Noel just sat there, eating. And then, when he had finished, he simply stood up and walked away. Liam followed his progress across the shiny airport floor with burning eyes. That exact scenario – Noel walking away from a seething Liam – would be re-enacted a lot over the next six months. It was Noel's new game plan. When Liam triggered off his temper, badly encroached upon his space and soul, Noel's inner voice said, Don't get mad, don't get even. Get walking.

*

A fleet of black cars awaited us from the Paddington train and they swept us towards the hotel in Exeter. This was not a flash joint by any standards, more a country-house retreat with old-fashioned furniture, creaking staircases. The staff, mainly female, tried to look nonplussed by the band's arrival but you could see in their eyes they had been waiting expectantly for this. They would have Oasis under their charge for two nights. At last, excitement.

The band checked in under different names, dumped their bags, swift cup of tea and then we were away again, the cars majestically sweeping out of the gravel driveway, dashing past the small group of young kids who loitered by the hotel entrance and stared at the group as if they were aliens.

We travelled in a convoy through pretty green and half an hour later we were inside the Westpoint Arena, a huge hall and so soulless. The group rushed to the stage and they soundchecked, then strolled outside for a photo call.

They made a few derisory comments to inane press questions, didn't really bother to pose and then walked haughtily back inside the venue. These pictures and quotes would appear on the cover of every major paper the following day.

Millions of people would see them. Must have taken all of ten minutes, start to finish.

*

Later on, when the crowd came down and I was just about to do the same, Liam stood by the barriers dancing around to the music blasting through the speakers. Somehow the crowd looked everywhere but towards him, and Liam looked genuinely happy.

*

First gig over. Noel is in the hotel bar. It's small. Comfy chairs and oak tables, a fireplace nearby. He is talking to two couples who are hotel residents. Introductions and compliments over, Noel asks one of the women, 'So what do you do?'

'Oh,' she dismissively says, 'it wouldn't interest you. Not you.' She laughs self-consciously and shakes her head. You, interested in my life? No, not you.

But Noel is determined. 'I am interested. Come on, what do you do? You don't work for fucking Blur or something, do ya?' Noel breaks into laughter. Then quickly stops. 'You don't, do you?' he seriously enquires. The woman is in her mid-thirties, dark-haired, still attractive. But shy.

'I'm a hairdresser,' she announces and then quickly adds, 'See, I told you it was boring, that it didn't matter.'

Noel considers her and then says quite simply, 'I don't care if you're a hairdresser. I really fucking don't. Just as long as you want to be the best hairdresser ever. See, that's all that counts in life. Being the best at what you do.' The woman now looks at Noel with real intrigue in her eyes. She had never imagined such sentiment in him.

The crafty magpie. Noel spots that the barman has stupidly vacated his position behind the bar. A light goes on in Gallagher's head. He glances round, stands and then darts behind the counter, picks up two bottles of champagne. Just as he's racing back to his seat the manager unexpectedly walks in. Noel stops, then quickly says, 'I was going to buy them.' But he sounds how he looks. Totally unconvincing. The manager makes a face as if to say, 'Sure you were' and Noel blurts out, 'I was. Really, I was. How much are they anyway?'

The manager tells him. The sum is in the hundreds. Noel looks at the bottles and then his voice shoots right up the scale. '*How much?* You're joking, aren't you? Fuck that.' He quickly goes behind the bar, puts them back.

'It's OK, mate, I'll leave it.'

Noel starts to walk back to his seat. The manager nods and leaves the bar. At which point, Noel stops, turns, nips back behind the bar, picks up a pint glass and, checking the manager really has gone, proudly announces to the assembled: 'Right, who wants a pint?' He draws two drinks before moving swiftly and rather triumphantly back to his seat.

*

Guigsy and Noel come to my room for further drinks. One of the guys downstairs had got over-friendly, grabbed Guigsy's drink. Guigsy snatched his arm, held it like a vice. 'Where I'm from, mate,' he said, 'you die for less.' The guy understood, backed off instantly.

Now Guigsy and I are listening to Noel, who is complaining drunkenly about the flak he's been getting for meeting Tony Blair at Number Ten.

'I went and had drinks with the Labour Government,' he says as if it was the most normal thing in the world. 'That's the party we've been trying to get into power the last billion years in case no one's fucking noticed.' His voice is slightly bitter. He's addressing his detractors. Not us. 'Anyway, give a shit. He's changing things.'

*

The second Exeter gig was better than the previous night's. The band were starting to gel now. The crowd's reaction was solid. Encouraging. And if the set list proved one thing it was that the quality of the *Be Here Now* songs was nowhere as poor as their detractors would have it. The title track, 'It's Getting Better, Man' and 'Stand By Me' especially, were easily outstripping the recorded versions. These songs were starting to burn, catching a lot of people's attention.

'I bet that gig,' Noel said, cooling down now in the dressing room, 'will get at least – oh – two out of ten in the *NME*.' And he was right. I get a lift with Guigsy back to the hotel. All day I have been hungover, attacked by hot flushes. No fucking around tonight. No late-night rantings.

Guigsy gets his driver to put on a Lee Perry CD. Guigsy is currently fascinated by this diminutive reggae genius and his music. 'Played this at rehearsals,' he says of one Perry tune. 'Liam on drums, me on bass.'

'Liam on drums?'

'Yeah, man, he's all right. Mike Rowe did a bit of keyboards. Top. First time I heard "D'You Know What I Mean?" I went, "Dub bass line for that". And "Wonderwall". And, believe it or not, "Live Forever".'

*

I make it downstairs at about ten for coffee and cigarettes. Liam is half pissed in the bar. Actually, forget the half. Then Bonehead walks in and Liam, vexed and worried, shouts over to him, 'I'm fucked.'

'Why?' Bonehead asks. Concerned.

'I got my Amex card bill. Twenty grand. Twenty fucking grand!'

'On what?' Bonehead sits, fumbles for his ciggies.

'That fucking holiday [a yacht trip in France with Patsy and friends]. Twenty grand. Twenty fucking grand.' Liam repeats the sum like a mantra, and now a hotel employee summons him to reception for a phone call. When he gets back the mantra has changed. And so has Liam's expression. It has considerably darkened. 'Fucking hell! Get on this. I got it wrong. It's 48 grand. Forty-eight fucking grand. Can you believe it? Can you fucking believe it? If my mates heard about this they'd kill me. Three years ago I was on the dole. A hundred quid a month. Now it's 48 grand, 48 fucking grand.'

He sounded amazed like a stunned general counting his dead after losing the battle. Then that familiar defiance reared up. 'Fuck it, man. I don't care about money. Not in it for the money. Fuck it.' Liam paused, took a long sip of his drink, placed his glass on the table, looked at me and said, 'But 48 grand, 48 fucking grand. Jesus.'

*

Noel once said onstage in New York just before playing 'Wonderwall', 'This is the song that bought us the houses and the cars and all that shit.' And all that shit.

*

Half an hour later Guigsy entered the bar. It was now about eleven and Liam was three sheets to the wind and full steam ahead. 'We're just silhouettes,' he confided to the bass player. 'Shadows. I know it's big what we're doing and I know all that, but fuck it, we are shadows, man. Silhouettes. That's it. Silh-o-uette. Top word, that, like that word. If I come back as a black chick, that's what I'm calling my band, The Silh-o-uettes. Fuck The Supremes. Silhouettes, that's the one. Right, innit?' He looked around for confirmation and everyone nodded their head in agreement. For the easy life, especially first thing in the morning.

*

A private plane. Today we travel from Exeter to Newcastle on a private plane. I'm intrigued. I've never travelled on a specially hired plane. But this is no Led Zep or U2 luxurious vehicle. There are no champagne bottles or caviar dishes on board. This is not the place for excess, largesse. This is a basic 30-seater plane mainly used by Tottenham Hotspur Football Club, with a pleasant enough stewardess doling out tea and biscuits while Guigsy has a crafty spliff in the back seat.

When we land in Newcastle the cars are waiting on the airstrip. As we walk towards them, Danny, Bonehead's security guard, says, 'I gobbed on one of the seats.' I look at him quizzically. 'Fucking Tottenham plane,' he explains. Classy kind of guy.

*

On the way into the hotel, Liam is still pissed. It's the best time to talk. In front of a tape recorder Liam clams up. Tight. But drunk, he has no qualms about shouting his mouth off. 1-2-3. On death: 'If I was two inches away from death I'd have it, man. Go for it. Go that two inches. How top would that be? Death! Come on.'

'You're not frightened of it?'

'Of what? What is there to be scared of? You can't be scared of something you don't know. Death might be top. So why shit it?'

On America: 'It's just money. That's why all the bands go there. Money. I know there's people out there who get it and fair enough, we should play for them. But it ain't any different to anywhere else. It's a big fucking world. Pakistan, man. We should play there. Have them over.'

*

After the first Newcastle show on Tuesday 16 September at the Newcastle Arena, we watch Celtic ('the only team of mine that is in a Premiership table,' Noel comments morosely) versus Liverpool in the dressing room. No one is talking about the gig, even though it was excellent. Everyone is fixed on the game. Liam goes to the toilet and when he comes back he looks admiringly at the large table in front of him, untidily strewn with newspapers, beer cans, discarded cigarettes. Dirty ash and cold chips. Everywhere. 'Look at that,' he admiringly says. 'A proper fucking Manc table. Top.'

*

When the game finishes, a programme about two explorers walking the Antarctic comes on. Noel turns excitedly to Mark Coyle, who has just arrived with Phil Smith. 'Did you see that story about the geezer who sacked his mate when they tried to walk to the Pole? Fucking top. They got about halfway there and it went right off between them. Stuck together for three weeks and then they get right into it one night. Big fucking kick-off. So this guy left his mate behind. Both of them went off in different directions and then one of the geezers gets frost-bite and has to have his foot cut off. And all because his mate dumped him.'

Noel was warming to his theme now. 'Can you imagine it if me and our kid did it. ''E' are, Liam, let's walk to the North Pole with tennis racquets for shoes. Two days later – what did you say, you cunt? Right, I'm off. Fuck the blizzard, I'm gone.'

'Yeah,' Liam put in plaintively, 'and I'd be walking 40 yards behind you, going, "Ah, come on, I was only joking.'''

*

The next night we watch a Marc Bolan documentary. He's a hero of Noel's, but when the late musician shows up on screen wearing a feather boa and talking to Cilla Black, Noel jumps up and walks away. 'I'm not fucking having that,' he clucks in disgust. 'Get the car, I'm off.' Someone in the programme says, 'The trouble with Marc was all the sycophants around him,' and Liam shouts out, 'Tell us something new.' Everyone who is not in the group uneasily shifts inside.

*

This time I travel back to the hotel with Bonehead, early Led Zeppelin blasting through the speakers. Liam's car is in front. He's travelling with Marcus Russell, who has already been quietly fuming over the reviews which are now coming in. 'Condescending cunts,' the manager says of the *NME*.

Bonehead is talking me through Zeppelin's history when we see the car ahead signal to pull over. 'Piss stop,' Bonehead shouts. The three of us relieve ourselves on the grass bank as cars flash by, screaming. 'We've got Led Zep on in our car,' Bonehead shouts to Liam. 'What have you got on in yours?'

'Fuck all. Me and Marcus are discussing the future.'

'What's it look like?' I ask.

'It looks like me, you dick.'

Then Liam Gallagher jumps back into his car and is whisked away.

Another plane, this time to Aberdeen. Cars wait on the tarmac in the relentless rain. The hotel is again located deep in the countryside. Later that night a mini van is hired and we venture into the village, to a local pub.

As we travel there, Noel shouts to Mark Coyle, 'Coyley, it's like the old days in this van.' But it never will be, not now.

At the boozer, the guys act tough, pretend nothing is happening. Oasis are at the bar. So what? But the girls have no qualms, no airs of coolness about them. They quickly come over. Friendly smiles; friendly people. So now the guys saunter over. 'All right?' 'You playing in town soon?'

Names are put on the guest list, autographs are signed. But the crush of people wanting to talk, to touch, gets on top. We leave in a hail of salutes and goodbyes. It's like this everywhere they go and they both love and regret it.

*

Later that night I sit with Mark Coyle and discuss Noel's songwriting, his prolific nature and how songs he wrote years and years ago are only now surfacing. 'Fucking amazing writer,' Coyley says, 'and just think of what's to come. It's outrageous.' This man was Noel's first songwriting partner. They made House tunes together until Noel started coming round his yard with songs such as 'She's Electric' or 'Live Forever'. Later on, after Noel joined the band, he brought in Coyley to set up the equipment in the rehearsal studio, asked him to monitor their live sound. Coyley worked every Oasis gig until Slane Castle. Then his ear started packing up, so he withdrew. No one knew it, least of all him, but later on in the tour and on the other side of the world, he would be back working with them.

In the morning Noel and I go out shopping. For records and clothes.

As we get in the car, Noel asks, 'What were you and Coyley talking about last night?'

'Noel Gallagher: songwriter, human or alien? Discuss.'

'And the verdict?'

'You're an alien,' I say, looking to pass on a kind of compliment. A swift, disgruntled look passes over Noel's face. I feel uncomfortable. That's what you get for trying to play clever and bump up someone's ego.

*

The first night at Aberdeen was good but the second show, on Saturday 20 September at the Aberdeen Exhibition and Conference Centre, was one of the finest gigs I've ever seen Oasis perform. They were sensational. I don't know what caused it but it was one of those rare but magical nights when it all joins up, when audience and band connect and push each other to the stars. Higher and higher. That was the gig we got. Band and audience joined at the hip and dancing the blues away. Life-affirming stuff. The music smashed into you, washed away all your wrongs, cleansed your soul. Reminded you why you made all this dedication in the first place.

Inspired. That's how I felt. So did the band. So did the crowd. It was breathless stuff. Afterwards Liam said, 'When the sound onstage is right and the crowd's like that I don't care, man, we'll beat anyone. Beatles, Who, Hendrix. I walked out onstage tonight and it was yes! Come on!'

Liam dedicated 'Wonderwall' to Noel that night. That's how good it was.

There was a posse from London – Meg, Patsy, the drum and bass man Goldie, others – and an all-night bar awaiting the band. Goldie had brought with him the tape of his tune 'Temper', the song Noel had plastered guitar all over. His playing was fractured, bruised. Goldie, large, vociferous, sporting heavy rings, jumped around. He shouted, 'Check it, man, check that guitar. Wild! Wild!'

Noel smiled, slightly embarrassed. The contradiction. Public displays don't come easy to him. But he can perform for thousands, alone with just a guitar as a friend.

*

At one point I sat with Bonehead. I told him my problem; how to put such a gig into words. Always the writer's dilemma, this, the distillation of this magic into a written meaning that matches its power. Music dissolves words. Every time. He replied, 'You write this. Oasis at Aberdeen were unbelievable. Now.' And then he screamed at the top of his lungs, 'WHO WANTS IT NEXT?'

And then at their next gig in Sheffield they played like saps.

*

Again the hotel was located in deep country, large, imposing but isolated. The band groaned when they arrived, when they saw this castle with its ancient corridors, its dark furniture. They liked to be in the centre of town, in the thick of things. They wanted to be near neon lighting. And although it wasn't hard to understand why such places had been booked for them – to avoid the prying media for one thing – Oasis on tour wanted to be near the action.

Noel and Meg booked in, but within half an hour had picked up their bags and gone to join the road crew at their hotel a lot nearer Sheffield town centre.

Meanwhile the rest of us gathered in the large dining room for food. Bonehead offered me wine but I refused. Too hungover from Aberdeen excess. 'Lightweight,' Bonehead shouted. 'Have some wine. Do you good.'

'Not tonight. Early night tonight.'

'Lightweight, lightweight!' Alan White tauntingly said.

'It won't be an early night for you,' Bonehead threatened. 'Not a chance.'

'What does "lightweight" mean?' the bar girl serving us innocently asked.

I finished up and went to my room, settled into bed. I didn't hear the 20 people whispering outside, I didn't see the door slowly opening. What I did see was Bonehead and Danny running into the room and jumping on top on me, followed by the rest of the party. 'Bundle,' someone shouted. With the weight of 20 people on top of me all I remember is slowly turning my head to see the bar maid at the foot of the bed jabbing her finger at me and shouting, 'Lightweight! Lightweight!' Guess she understood its meaning now.

The next day she told me, 'You were dead lucky, you know. The original plan was to come in, strip you naked, carry you outside and lock all the doors. Then they were going to ring the police and tell them that there was a mad naked fan outside haranguing the group . . .'

*

Later that afternoon, in the vast Sheffield Arena, I find Noel in the canteen, eating. 'Guess what? Supernova Heights has been burgled. The cops reckon they've been coming in for weeks and taking stuff. I knew something was up when Meg couldn't find her sheepskin coat. Still, good news: they deliberately left something behind.'

'What was that?'

"The book you wrote on us.'

'Ha ha ha. How did they get in?'

'Well, Meg reckons they came in through that catflap on the back door.' I tried to imagine a grown man squeezing through about five inches of space and as I struggled with that image, Noel read my mind and exclaimed, 'Birds! What can you do?'

*

Prince Naseem Hamed, Sheffield born and bred and so much smaller than you'd expect (but aren't all celebs?), attended both shows. There were obvious comparisons between the boxer and Oasis – huge talent backed up by grandiose statements, daily charges of arrogance – and of course, Liam was not going to have him take centre stage. 'How much dosh you get for a fight?' he enquired.

'Enough,' replied Naseem.

'For a million pounds I'd fight you. And I'd deck you.' Everyone laughed. But Liam.

*

The worst bit was the waiting. Soundcheck completed, meal eaten, if the hotel wasn't in striking distance the band were forced to make their own entertainment. For Liam that usually meant drinking. Anything to help shatter the silence, break the boredom.

Mike Rowe entered the dressing room with his brother. His nickname was now Austin Powers and it wasn't hard to see why. It was the slim frame, the large glasses and the curly hair. The keyboard player said to Liam, 'I've got a tape of this track I've been working on. Do you want to hear it?'

'Fucking right I do,' Liam exclaimed. 'Put it on, right now. I'm bored off my tits here.'

'Here we go then, squire,' Mike cheerfully announced, jamming the tape into the machine. Yet he still looked uneasy, as if he was taking some kind of risk here. And then I understood why. The track was an instrumental. A minute in and Liam, who had been carefully listening, looked up and snapped at him, 'Where's the fucking singing?'

'There isn't any,' Mike quickly explained.

'Well, turn this shit off. I want to hear songs, man. Not you going doodly-fucking-doo on your fucking keyboard. Songs, man. Where's the fucking song, you dick?' Mike retrieved his tape, silently left the room. Liam reached for a bottle.

*

On their last visit here, in 1995, when Oasis were still on the rise, that thrilling period of mayhem and success, barriers had been erected between band and crowd.

Liam got real annoyed at the distance this created. He said to the crowd, 'If you want to get closer to us, fuck those guards off and come here.'

Hundreds of kids vaulted the barriers and rushed forward. 'It was like the fucking revolution,' a flushed Noel Gallagher said afterwards. Tonight, years later, that rebel spirit was absent. The band played in the most perfunctory way and the crowd stood and stared, as if they were witnessing something above them – not of them. Before, they looked straight at the band. Now they looked up to them. That's how it felt.

'Well, that was a load of shit,' Noel said after the first night's show. He was standing outside the dressing room, flu coursing through his veins. As Naseem had an important fight coming up, he wasn't allowed near the boxer. 'Thrown out of my own dressing room,' Noel muttered. 'I might as well pack up and go home to feed the cats for the rest of my life.'

Opposite him there was a room that contained after-show guests. One of them was Garry Blackburn, the Oasis plugger who promotes their records for TV and radio. He looked concerned. 'They're putting out "All Around The World" as the third single,' he explained. 'But Noel is refusing to edit it down. I can't take it in at the moment at nine minutes long, no one will play it. Unless something happens they're going to have the first flop of their career.' A flop? The word would never have been uttered six months ago.

*

In the car on the way back to the hotel, Liam announced his choice of producer for the next Oasis album. Paul Weller. 'I don't want to be his mate or his brother or anything like that. I'm Noel Gallagher's brother and that'll do me. Plus Weller means too much to me, but he should do the job. It'd be top. We'd set up and play and he can turn the buttons and try and make sense of it all. Imagine it. Us and Weller. In the same studio. It would be like the Birmingham Six set free all over again.'

*

In the hotel bar that night some guests joined the table, asked about *Be Here Now*. Liam and Bonehead couldn't resist it. 'See,' Liam announced, 'what you don't know is that man's first recorded words were "Won Ereh Eb". Now we only found this out the other day, didn't we, Bone?'

'That's right.' The guitarist then curled his mouth around the words "Won Ereh Eb", pronouncing them with dutiful care. The guests, two men, three girls, stared hard at the pair, hung onto their every word. 'So get on this,' Liam interjected. 'Spell "Won Ereh Eb" backwards. It's "Be Here Now".'

'And I swear to God,' Bonehead put in, 'we didn't know that when the album came out. Amazing, isn't it?'

"That's amazing,' one of the guys said, looking to his companions, who all nodded their heads. Liam and Bonehead both took big sips of their drinks, put the glasses down on the table with a sigh and then the two musicians and friends decided they couldn't keep it up any longer. And they burst out laughing. Twelve hours later we had all been driven back to London.

*

At the mixing desk, situated in the middle of the huge Earls Court arena, Liam Gallagher exchanged greetings with Huw, the band's sound engineer. Huw had taken over when the injury to Coyley's ear occurred. Lately he had been getting a lot of flak. Marcus and others were complaining that the gigs were too loud. 'It's fucking Oasis,' Huw pointed out. 'They're *meant* to be heard loud.'

Marcus saw it differently. He explained, "What you have to remember is that when kids come along to these shows they want to sing along to the songs. They can't do that if the music is at such a volume it's hurting them.'

Commerce versus instincts. The issue would never successfully be resolved.

*

For the Earls Court shows, Oasis's old friends The Verve were playing support. The press had spent weeks building up this pairing as a battle of the bands, a fight for the *numero uno* slot, a battle for the heart and soul of the country. That week the *NME*'s front cover was taken up by shots of both bands and a huge article inside discussing their merits. I told Liam this and he looked at me in disgust. 'They're our mates. It's music. What the fuck are they on about?' Then he quickly walked away.

*

Noel comes up to the seats reserved for guests and the handicapped and watches The Verve. He refuses all requests for autographs until after the band has finished. He watches The Verve like a hawk. And at the conclusion of their set, with Richard Ashcroft screaming at the audience to 'Come on!', Noel rises to his feet and gives them a standing ovation.

*

After their first show, where he again dedicated 'Live Forever' to Diana, Liam got in a strop about something and briskly exited. 'The singer has left the building,' Noel cried cheerfully.

*

Backstage Noel was buzzing on the high he had received from the show. He drank copious amounts of beer, challenged all who made it into the dressing room to a game of pool. One of these people was a representative for the Liverpool dockers, a guy called John. 'When I did that thing at Number Ten,' Noel confided in him, 'I said to Blair, What about the dockers? and he said, We'll look into it.'

John replied, 'That's what I can't understand. The Government has got a 51 per cent stake in the docks. Now when it's the Tories you understand them trying to shaft you. But this is a Labour government.'

'Tell you what,' Noel said. 'We record all the shows. We'll give you a track for that benefit album from tomorrow's gig.'

'You're joking,' John replied.

'No, not at all.'

And he gave them 'Don't Look Back In Anger'.

*

Meanwhile Kevin, Noel's then security guard, sat outside the room waiting for his client to tire out enough that he could accompany him home. He looked glum. He knew it would be a long night. And he was right.

*

In the dressing room the next day, Noel played through a cassette of the b-sides for 'Stand By Me', the second single from *Be Here Now*. But the title track wasn't what interested him. It was the track 'Going Nowhere' that excited him. On it Noel had used muted trumpets, soft keyboards, a definite nod to Burt Bacharach. The lyrics concerned the greed of the music business. And the melody was a killer. When it finished, Noel looked up and said, 'Not bad for a washed-up songwriter, eh, chaps?'

*

Laser pencils plagued the band throughout the tour. Fans' had started gleefully shining them on their sweating foreheads as the band played onstage. Oasis hated it. They could feel this light on them but could do nothing to stop it. It rendered them powerless. It also made them uneasy. They felt like targets. Security guards such as Terry were instructed to rush into the dark, heaving audience to grab the offenders.

But it was a fruitless task. Such vast numbers defeated them every time.

In the end, Gareth, the onstage monitor engineer, would make an announcement before the band's entrance. He said the band would walk if anyone used a laser beam on them. Then, at Earls Court, someone shone one on Noel's forehead. 'Oi! Cunty bollocks!' the songwriter raged into the microphone. 'I hope your house gets burnt down to the ground, you lose your job and someone shags your bird, you fucking wanker!' Liam looked admiringly at his older brother, said to the offender in admonishing tones, 'You've had it now, I'm telling you, you've had it now.'

*

Halfway through each set, Liam would saunter offstage and Noel would sing two songs, 'Magic Pie' and 'Don't Look Back In Anger'. Usually Liam exited stage right but on the second night he wandered stage left to the seats that had been erected for close friends and family. He was dressed in all white. He skipped into a row, casually spoke with an aunt, kissed his mum, went over and sat and cuddled with Patsy and then, as Noel was finishing 'Anger', gave his wife a little kiss before strolling back to the stage to sing for 17,000 people as if he was just out to buy some milk and would be back from the shops in a minute. I don't know if this was a carefully staged act. Probably was. But it worked a treat. The boy oozed class.

*

Channel 4's Teletext service, plus several papers, reported that the residents of Earls Court were trying to ban Oasis from playing the venue ever again. They blamed the fans. Acts such as Phil Collins and Take That were fine, no problem. They attracted a nice class of person. But Oasis fans? One resident said, 'They're scumbags. They urinate in your garden, dump rubbish on your door and openly buy drugs from dealers in the street.'

*

It was Monday, comedown day, the day we caught the train to Birmingham.

'I know this is probably a stupid question,' Noel said in the dressing room of the city's NEC Arena, 'but has anyone seen our kid.' Oasis had soundchecked without him, not an unusual occurrence. Liam seldom attended soundchecks. They bored him. Today it was the week-end excesses that was preventing Liam from appearing on time. Apparently, after the first Earls Court show he had been driven home swiftly. 'Twenty minutes after coming offstage,' he beamed, 'and I was standing in the kitchen in my leopard-skin pyjamas making spaghetti hoops on toast. Fucking top. Fuck rock'n'roll.' Yeah, fuck rock'n'roll. But the next night he went out partying.

'You ever had them pink E's?' Liam enquired. 'Well, they're shit. Everyone started crumbling around me. I was left alone howling at the moon. Good night, though.'

Yeah, so long live rock'n'roll. Then.

*

At the soundcheck, Noel led the band through two new songs. One was a straight-ahead rocker with a Led Zep-type riff burning through it. The second had a swirling guitar line which Noel endlessly repeated. In the dressing room afterwards they listened to the tapes.

'Listen to that rundown,' Mike Rowe said admiringly of his own playing. Noel turned on him with a sneer. 'You mean that tiny bit of music which I've made into an epic,' he asked. He said it with such venom that all went quiet. Mike had unwittingly strayed onto Noel's turf. And the lion had roared back.

*

At Birmingham's NEC Arena Liam came offstage halfway through and complained of his performance: 'It's not right. I'm not pissed enough.'

*

For 'Champagne Supernova', Steve Cradock was invited onstage to play guitar. That made him the second-ever musician to be invited by Oasis to join them onstage. The first was John Squire at Knebworth.

Meanwhile, down the front, loads of kids were being taken to the First Aid tent for recovery. The crush of the crowd. 'Take it easy down there,' Noel said into his mike. 'We don't want you dying.' Then he paused and joked, ''Cos then you won't buy a T-shirt.'

*

Guigsy stood in the dressing room fuming at the heavy-handed approach of the bouncers, the lax security measures. Steve Allen, who worked as an advance security guard and looked after crowd security, stood with him. 'It's a fucking gig,' Guigsy said. 'No one should fucking die for it.' His words carried a lot of weight. You rarely saw him angry, rarely saw him raging. When he left, there was silence. Then Steve said, 'I'm not just saying this but I have never worked for a band who care so much about their fans.'

I believe he didn't say it for my benefit.

Iggy, an old friend of the band, shows up at the gig. He brings tales from Manchester of girls leaving their guys to go off with their best friends. There are other stories of their mutual friends, court appearances, burglaries, drunken squabbles, nights in police cells and the like.

Meanwhile Noel has spread out the eight pairs of Kicker shoes he has somehow acquired and is standing there admiring them. 'Imelda fucking Marcos has got nothing on me,' boasts the man who escaped.

*

At the hotel afterwards, Ocean Colour Scene's bass player, Damon Minchella, comes over for a drink. He triumphantly says to Liam, 'Next week The Verve will go in at number one in the album charts. That means the charts, the top three, will be Verve, Oasis and Ocean Colour Scene. How about that? Phil Collins? You can fuck right off.'

'It's like the '60s,' Liam points out. 'Beatles, Stones and Who.' Then he says quietly, 'I can go now. I've done what I was put on this earth to do.'

It wouldn't be the last time on this tour that Liam would speak of going.

*

Noel Gallagher sits in the downstairs den of Supernova Heights, silently fuming. There is a break in the tour and I had gone round to watch football. I got the Dutch courage in and asked him what the fuck Oasis were doing playing a benefit gig for Princess Diana in Paris. That ain't rock'n'roll, that's suicide.

'That was fucking Liam dedicating "Live Forever" 11 nights on the bounce,' he sourly explains. 'I tell you, man, I cringed every time he said it and because he said it the media have gone, Well, what are you going to do about it? So now we're playing a gig for her. It's fucking wrong.'

'So fuck off the media.'

'I can't.'

'Why not?'

'Because it's too much hassle.'

'Really?'

It was why Liam felt sympathy for Diana. He too had been chased in cars.

And it was why Noel would not fuck with the pressmen. He knew their ability to make a day feel like a year. So damn him and his situation but he was too tired to play the game now. The grief outweighed the fun.

'I can't go through with it,' he admitted. 'I just can't be arsed. But I tell you, man, I'm on the road for the next year and than after that I'm shutting Oasis down. I've got 35 songs at the moment and I don't need to do this. I'm going to wait until people are gagging for another record. I'm going to take two years off and do fuck all. That's for sure.'

Another Gallagher brother talking about going. This was getting kind of contagious now. Maybe New York would be the place to even things out.

Two

YOUR TICKETS PLEASE
The Big Apple and Europe

True or false?

'Fame, this special kind of fame, feeds itself on outrage, on what the counselors of lesser men would consider bad publicity – hysteria in limousines, knife fights in the audience, bizarre litigation, treachery, pandemonium and drugs. Perhaps the only natural law attaching to true fame is that the famous man is compelled, eventually, to commit suicide.'

Don DeLillo, *Great Jones Street*

HOWEVER big and hardened they thought they were, America had a history of breaking Oasis. In two. Twice now Noel had bailed out and caught lonely planes back to London, exasperated and furious at Liam's behaviour. The fevered publicity surrounding these walk-outs always made Oasis seem ready to snap for good. Certainly, that was the American conception of the band.

Two childish brothers squabbling like fuck with an army of great songs behind them but an attitude that badly needed sorting out. This jaunt then was a let's-see-what-mess-we-left-behind-when-last-we-were-here-and-is-there-anything-we-can-do-about-it? kind of thing. The first half of this trip – I didn't accompany them – was purely promotional.

A round of media interviews to be finished off with two shows at New York's Hammerstein Ballroom, which is where I came in. The band would then return in January for a major tour. It was hoped by management and record company that all concerned would be on Sunday-best behaviour. No fights, no quarrels, no punch-ups.

*

'He's going to fucking get it tonight, the cunt.' Liam and Phil Smith have just walked into the dressing room of the Hammerstein Theatre and the singer is seething. 'Proper ruck between me and our kid coming up, proper fucking ruck.' Liam stalks the small dressing room endlessly. Yet, despite his dark utterances, I was glad to see him.

True, sometimes you do have to be on your guard with him, for he can snap in the most unlikely places. But Liam Gallagher also has a lot of things going for him. He's surprisingly thoughtful, always the one band member that checked I was OK for a lift to the hotel. He's funny, lives with a wit that borders on classic surrealism. But today he wasn't joking around. Today Noel had upset him by walking out of an interview. Today Liam wanted revenge.

'All you people,' he sneered at me, 'telling him how great he fucking is, you just don't know. He's a right cunt. He is. But everyone's too busy telling him how top he is. If only you knew,' Liam said conspiratorially, as if he was privy to some dark secret that he kept close to his chest and would one day let loose to cause all kinds of carnage.

When Liam was in this mood there was no room for argument, no room to reply. His fury closed spaces off. The sound of Noel soundchecking, singing 'Magic Pie' in fact, came faintly through the walls. Liam stopped talking and he listened, intently. Then he said, 'He sings like that fucking bird from M People. "Think of me,"' he crooned in a prissy female voice, '"Yeah, I've got my magic pie." Dick. You wait. I'm going to fucking do him.' And he nodded his head. And he waited.

*

For Oasis, New York meant shopping. Especially these days with endless amounts of money to draw upon. Clothes and records, sure. But toys were their thing. They came back laden with all the latest gadgets and then went out again to buy suitcases to fit them all in. They all had kids to remember back home. Theirs and other people's. But really they were just pleasing the kid inside them.

*

In the dressing room Alan White, to pass the time of day, innocently asked, 'Where's Liam?' and Noel brutally snapped back, 'As far away from here as possible because if I see him I'm going to punch him right out.'

Dead silence.

*

Alec McKinlay from Ignition, Oasis's management company, arrives from London. He wants to see Noel as soon as possible. 'I think you're going to have to prepare yourself for a media storm in the UK,' he tells him.

'Why?' Noel says. 'What have I said now?' There is an amused expression on his face. Noel recognizes that it's not everyone who is warned about media storms coming their way.

'You gave some interview to the *Toronto Sun* where you said people should stop whining about Diana's death.'

'Yeah? And?'

'Look, I agree with everything you said, but somebody from Reuters has put it on the wire and it will probably be front-page news tomorrow.'

Noel stood up, stretched. 'Give a shit,' is what he said.

*

'You've got to see this guy –'

On the street near the hotel a homeless man sat slumped against the wall. His placard read: 'Please give me money.

For drugs, alcohol and prostitutes.' Noel told me, 'Look at his collection box.' It was full up with grimy dollars.

*

What happened was that Noel and Liam sat down for an interview and the first question the guy asked was: 'What do you think of *Mr Bean*?' And Noel thought, What the fuck has that got to do with *Be Here Now*? The second question was: 'If your wife was to have kids, would she scream?' So Noel said, '"E' are, mate, I'm going. And you can fuck right off.' But Liam said, 'No, stay.' But what the fuck for? is what Noel wanted to know. 'You spend seven months making an album, putting everything you got into it, and then you come out and they ask you about *Mr Bean* and your missus.' Doesn't make too much sense over here, either.

*

At the first soundcheck Liam played drums while Noel sang Neil Young's 'Hey Hey My My,' and completely ignored him. At the second soundcheck, Liam didn't even bother to show up. Both gigs were excellent, but Noel and Liam deliberately avoided each other. They nearly collided on the cramped stairway while watching support act Fun Loving Criminals, but again Noel walked away.

Onstage they remained tight-lipped, uncommunicative. Songs were briskly announced, banter was kept at a very low level. Both nights the band did a runner from the gig not bothering to stay behind and meet various well-wishers.

Noel and Liam, and their wives, took separate cars. And somewhere along the way this line of non-communication was broken. I wasn't privy to how they resolved the angry space between them but by the time it came to record 'Don't Go Away' (the US single) for David Letterman's prestigious TV show the next day, the argument had faded and no punches were thrown.

*

In the dressing room of *The David Letterman Show* Noel turns to Marcus and says, 'Have we got some time off soon?'

'Yes,' Marcus says, expansively. 'About a day.'

Actually they have two weeks before they leave for the European leg of the tour. But first they must record two b-sides for 'All Around The World', which their producer to date, Owen Morris, has now agreed to edit.

They are due in Ridge Farm Studios, in Surrey, on Monday. 'What's the day today?' Noel asks.

'Thursday,' Alec McKinlay replies.

'What songs we doing?' Liam asks.

'New songs,' Noel says. 'Well, actually one new song and a cover.' He stops to consider his work schedule. 'So I've got four days to write a song.' Noel looks serious for about 20 seconds and then he brightens up. 'Fuck it,' he goes, 'two covers it is then.'

*

When we got back to London, Guigsy just had time to grab his bags and dash to the hospital before his wife Ruth gave birth to their first child, a son, Patrick. Then he went home. Then he was back on the road.

*

Noel Gallagher, in his downstairs den, is again silently fuming. He has just played me 'Flashbax', one of the two songs – The Stones' 'Street Fighting Man' is the other – that Oasis have just recorded for the b-side of 'All Around The World'. (Another song, 'The Fame', is already recorded and will appear on all formats. 'Street Fighting Man' is the same except for the vinyl 12-inch version.) Noel sings

'Flashbax'. He didn't want to but he was forced to. Liam was 'incapacitated'.

'He came down,' complains Noel, 'and went on the piss for two whole days. Then he turned round and said, "I can't sing, my throat is too fucked". I mean, why the fuck does he do it?' He must have been through situations like this a million times but the songwriter still seemed genuinely puzzled by his sibling's errant behaviour. I tell Noel, 'I guess it's to get at you, but it's also to do with the fact that if anyone tells him A then he naturally goes to B.'

'But he's 24, for fuck's sake. C'mon. Grow up.'

'Grow up? He can't do that because he sees that as a weakness.'

'I know and it pisses me right off.'

'But it's also what makes Oasis.'

'Yeah, I know, but I reckon we're losing it. I really do. I said to our kid the other day, you're boring. You really are. And so am I. And the trouble is Oasis have just got too safe. Things have got to change because everything is just far too safe.'

And that was the seed for the belligerent attitude Noel would now use to get him through the tour, the safe tour, the tour where for the first time work came first and play a very distant second.

*

On Monday 3 November 1997, on the Eurostar train to France, at about 11 o'clock, as English fields flashed by the window, Liam turned to Noel and said, 'Did you see that thing in the paper? Said you were worth 39 million quid.'

'Am I fuck,' Noel quickly responded. 'Do you think if I was worth 39 million I'd get up at seven in the morning to sit on a train with you shower of shit so that we can play to a load of French people? Fucking joking, mate. If I had that kind of dosh I'd have a robot built and send that out on the road while I lay on my arse all day drinking lager and watching the TV.'

Liam – who'd obviously been busy with the newsprint – turned to Guigsy.

'Here, Guigs,' he asked, 'did you see that dickhead Chris Hutton in the paper? [Hutton was the original singer of Rain with Guigs and Bonehead before being ousted to make way for Liam.] He said, "Guigs was my best mate until one day he just turned around and said, You're out. I haven't seen him since," and all this bollocks, the twat. You know what he also said? He said that he was the first singer in Oasis. Was he fuck! He was in Rain. Not Oasis. If he says that in his book then that's it, I'm having it injuncted. I am. He can't say that. He can't, can he?' He really was very aggrieved. Liam thought up the band's name. Oasis was his baby. And nobody else's. OK? (When Hutton's book was published, he did not claim to have been Oasis' lead singer.)

A press officer, Doe Phillips, has now joined the tour. Her job will be to set up daily interviews for Noel after sound-checks and organize his press conferences, at which Guigsy will accompany him. Noel loves talking and delivering his views on everything but, like so many musicians, he will, of course, spend all his time complaining that he has to talk so much to the press.

*

At the hotel, the Golden Tulip in Lille, Steve Cradock of Ocean Colour Scene, who were supporting on some of the dates, was already ensconced in the bar. Liam was swift to join him. Phil Smith was also present.

It was now about two in the afternoon. Liam told Cradock that Oasis had been recording, enthused big time about the Stones song they'd covered. 'When I saw the lyrics to "Street Fighting Man" I just went, This is the best song ever written. "My name is called disturbance." Fucking right it is. Top lyrics.'

'Yeah, but did you see what Keith Richards said about you in *Mojo*?' I asked. 'He said that although they might have been bad in the early days, you guys were just obnoxious. Now he's going to cop royalties off your cover version.'

'No,' Liam emphasized, 'no, no, get on this. We did that song after *that* interview came out. And we did that deliberately just to fuck him up even more.' Liam looked satisfied, drained his beer.

'Did you do any other tunes?' Cradock asked.

'Yeah, we did a song called "Flashbax", and get on this,' Liam announced, now determined to have everyone's attention, 'this is no word of a lie, on my mother's life this is. When I was about four or five my grandmother had this land, this is in Ireland like. Anyways, I was sitting in a field when I saw this glowing light.'

Cradock and I exchanged glances. Liam caught us. 'No,' he insisted, 'No lie this, right?'

We nod our heads, Liam continues.

'You know normally, like in films when a kid sees something and you're sitting there going, Run away, you daft fucker. Well, I know how that happens because I just thought, fuck it. So I walked towards it and as I did it just shot off. Bang. Gone. Now get on this. Me and Phil are down at Ridge Farm and we've gone out into the fields and what do I see but this same fucking fight and we've just recorded a song called "Flashbax" and I'm going to Phil, Fucking hell, I'm having a flashback. And then this herd of sheep started running around us.'

'It was like a white blanket,' Phil interjected, 'going round and round us.'

'Yeah, man,' Liam agreed. 'And we're just stood there going, This is top. I'm telling you, man, that was the best fucking night of my life. Without a doubt. The best night of my life.'

*

At around six that evening Liam rips open a bottle of Sheridan's and starts drinking. At seven-thirty he's standing by the DJ decks when his chest involuntarily heaves and he turns, retches and brings up the entire contents of his stomach. The sick is deposited on the floor by a flight case. Liam wipes his mouth and walks away. He's on-stage in three quarters of an hour.

The European tour opens with a gig dotted with great moments. These are 'Fade In/Out', 'D'You Know What I Mean?' and, strangely enough, because in my book it's a tune that has not stayed the course, 'Roll With It'. The venue is the smallest that the band have visited so far on this tour. France is a notoriously hard country for British acts to crack. But the crowd is warm, very enthusiastic.

After the gig Noel sits in the dressing room, moaning that there are no chemicals available. 'Have a good drink instead,' Bonehead advises. ('Good drink' has now been installed, along with 'Geezer!' and 'Lightweight!', as key tour words.)

'Of course I'm going to have a good drink,' Noel replies. 'And if you find any chemicals don't take any because the last time you took them you ended up throwing punches at lamp-posts.'

Then there was me and Noel and then Marcus came in and Noel went into one about the Welsh.

'I mean, what good fucking singers have you ever produced apart from daft little choirboys who go flying through the air without the greatest of ease?'

Always up for a verbal ruck, Noel.

'They've got Tom Jones,' I told him.

'You what? Tom Jones. Not you as well. I can't believe it. Tom fucking Jones. My my, Delilah!'

'Check out his version of "Mohair Sam". I'm telling you . . .'

'Mohair Sam? Who the fuck is Mohair Sam when he's at home. Nowhere man, more like it.'

And on. And on. And so on.

That week French lorry drivers went on strike and bought the entire country to a standstill. This meant that the Paris show – the dreaded Diana benefit – had to be cancelled. The band, equipment and stage show now had to be taken out of France and somehow moved into Spain. A nightmare for all involved, especially Michael O'Connor, the production manager, who saw everything literally dispersed around Europe. Amps in Germany, stage gear in Italy. Nice. He would later tell me that in one day he spent some 12 hours on the phone keeping track of everything.

The band meanwhile travelled to Paris by train to play a TV show. Marcus looked slightly worried. He had spoken to the insurance company bankrolling the tour. Following the Paris gig's cancellation, the company were now doing everything in their power to hold onto the money.

'They're saying the strike isn't as bad as we're saying,' Marcus revealed, 'because at home it's only the fourth item on the news.'

'Send them this,' Maggie, the tour manager, said, handing over a copy of the *Herald Tribune* which carried the story on the front page.

*

It was a miserable Paris we pulled into, a winter Paris where the relentless rain is blown into your face by an astringent wind and the grey buildings melt into grey skies. At least the hotel was plush, comfortable. And expensive. It was near the Champs-Élysées and that kind of living don't come cheap. I holed up in my room. Reading, writing and eating. I wasn't in the mood for games. Truth is, I had just met someone and she was colouring my mind.

Just as I was drifting into sleep I heard someone singing Tom Jones' 'It's Not Unusual' on the street outside. It was not Noel Gallagher. Of that we can be sure.

*

The band knew the French TV station Canal +, as the seasoned British writer Nick Kent had recently shot a documentary on them for transmission by the channel that month. Oasis were now here to perform versions of 'D'You Know What I Mean?' and 'Stand By Me'. The show itself was a mix of music and comedy.

Liam had been up all night and as the performance time beckoned he started getting nervous.

'I don't know if I can get the high notes,' he kept saying to no one in particular. Noel meanwhile had wandered out into the studio, where they were rehearsing a sketch about the truck drivers' strike using *Spitting Image*-style puppets. One of the technicians noticed him sitting alone and approached him. In broken English, he asked him what he made of the strike. Did he support it?

'I'm always there for a bit of "up the workers",' Noel cheerfully replied, 'but they could have left it to next week when the lads weren't in town.'

The French guy nodded thoughtfully and wandered off without the slightest clue whatsoever as to what Noel Gallagher had just said. Or where he stood on the strike.

*

The band perform their two songs and perform them well. Interestingly, Mike Rowe's keyboards are pushed well to the front, washing over the guitars and delivering

one clue at least as to where the future Oasis may sonic-
ally end up.

'I was in bits up there,' Liam said afterwards. 'Badly
crumbling. Done it good, though.' Then he looked around
nervously, just like a child who has realized he's got away
with it. 'Come on, let's go before I really do fuck it up.'

*

On the way home Phil Smith said to Noel, 'Your kid will
have his head right down tonight.'

'Yeah. He's been dead quiet today. He's been all right.
Still, one good kip and that will be it. He'll wake up as Mr
Annoying Cunt again.' Noel sighed as the car entered the
tunnel where Dodi and Diana died.

*

Musicians love moaning. Here's one of Noel's
complaints. No one ever questions him on dance or soul
music. Pisses him right off. No one asks, 'What do you
reckon? Jackson Five or Sly Stone?'

He spent three years in Manchester's clubs, E'd up and
giving it large on the dance floor – he even stopped playing guitar for a while, so taken was he by the scene – but
all to no avail. No one brings the subject up. So tonight
he is going to see Portishead and in the car I ask him the
question and what does he say? 'Sly Stone. Of course.'

*

We watch Portishead – who are excellent for at least
three quarters of their show – from a balcony. Every now
and then, as another loitering drum beat is started and
vocalist Beth's solemn but affecting voice comes floating
in, a pissed Noel punctures the reverential silence from
the audience by shouting, 'C'mon, give us a slow one.'

*

Afterwards we go to their dressing room. Noel meets Geoff Barrow and Beth Gibbons, the duo behind Portishead. Soon they're nattering away. I stand near and hear Noel tell Geoff – and I have no idea why – that he wants 'Strings Of Life' by Rhythim Is Rhythim played at his funeral. Geoff now mentions some of the lukewarm reviews that the last Portishead album has been receiving. Nodding his head vigorously, Noel tells him, 'Tell me about it. You're on the dole and you form a band 'cos you're bored off your tits. You write a load of songs and you get a deal. Then you put a record out and then you get some smart cunt come along and ask you what the fuck it's all about and you're sitting there going, Don't ask me, I don't fucking know!'

'Tell me about it,' says Geoff. And they both glance at me.

*

If they had regular jobs they would say, 'Yeah, let's go out for a drink or check this club one night.' But it's Noel Gallagher and Geoff Barrow. So it's 'Yeah, man, you have to play on my next record.'

On we go to another club. We leave Portishead behind. It's just Noel, Paul Stacey (now nicknamed Strangeboy), myself and Rob, Noel's personal security guard. (I know. Personal security guard. It sounds weird but there's literally millions of pounds riding on this Gallagher boy and no one wants to take any chances – hence the 24-hour protection.) And he's good, Rob, very good.

As we enter the club, a photographer's shark eyes light up. Then Noel and Strangeboy, badly pissed, go out on the dance floor to fuck around. Rob doesn't follow. Instead he places himself right in front of the guy, who has casually slipped his camera over his shoulder but has kept his head turned the other way. Rob later explains,

'A lot of them try this trick where they look one way but they've got their camera positioned and ready so all they're doing is just clicking away and no one suspects a thing because they're not looking at their subject. That's what that guy was up to.'

Rob used to live with the Aborigines. It shows.

*

Now Noel is on the Champs-Élysées, crouching down in the four a.m. light and bringing up his food. I go over and pat him on the shoulder.

'You all right, boss?'

'Fuck off, you cockney cunt.'

Then he bursts into laughter and then he retches again.

'No, Noel, are you OK?'

'Fuck off, you cockney cunt.'

Then he bursts into laughter and then he retches again. This scenario lasts for three minutes.

'Fuck off . . . cockney . . . Ha ha ha . . . Fuck off . . . cockney . . . Ha ha ha.'

Noel finally stands up and looks down at his mess. 'Fucking good night, eh?' he says, wiping his mouth with his sleeve. 'Sure was. You Manc c . . .'

*

I had one of those short sleeps where you awake with a start and ten minutes later realize you're still pissed. I go down to the foyer to pay my bills and bump into Liam. 'What did you do last night?' I ask him.

'Went to this bar across the road. It was fucking top. It's just across there. Come on. I'll show it to you.' Lager. Jack Daniel's. Breakfast.

An hour later and everyone has joined us in this roomy, cavernous bar. Apparently the night before the boys had caused a commotion just by being there. Liam wants the same excitement again, only there is no one here and it's now 11 in the morning. Today is travel day, Spain the destination. The talk is of suntans and sunshine and thank fuck we'll soon be playing music and away from all this ugly rain and wind.

Only Bonehead is without alcohol surging through his veins. He has woken up sober.

Maggie enters the bar, collects us together. She has worked with this band for years now, so is adept at hiding her worry that a group of well-inebriated guys will not be able to follow instructions on how to get to Spain. But any doubt is swiftly assuaged when we quickly drown our drinks *en masse* and eagerly jump into cars, enter the crazy slipstream of Paris traffic.

As we pass the Champs-Élysées, Noel puts his head out of the car, starts shouting, 'Good drink! Good drink!' at the rest of the entourage.

At the airport, more drinks. Bonehead now joins in. As we ease our hangovers, the drink now starts to take him in the upward direction. In astonishingly quick time his eyes turn wobbly, his speech slows, the spirit is upon him. Suddenly he grabs Noel's shades, Liam's hat and dons Terry's huge coat. ''E' are, 'e' are,' he roars, 'who the fuck is this?'

Then he starts impersonating Brian Harvey from East 17, jerking his body around, pretending to sing. Suddenly an armed guard walks by. Bonehead freezes. So does the guard's expression. Both men eye each other warily. And then Bonehead looks down. At the man's gun. And he gives him the most friendly smile in the world.

On the plane Noel tells Liam to order a Bloody Mary. 'Top fucking drink, you'll love it.'

'Nah, man, I ain't drinking that shit.'

'Why not?'

''Cos it's shit.'

'Oh, you've had loads, have you?'

As they start sniping at each other, as the surrounding businessmen start ruffling their newspapers, start looking a little nervous, I see the stewardess size up the situation. Then she slowly and slyly pushes the drinks trolley out of sight. I hear the unmistakable clink of bottles being removed. Then she reappears.

'What would you like to drink, sir?' she sweetly asks Noel.

'I'll have a Bloody Mary,' Noel answers, eagerly rubbing his hands together.

'A Bloody Mary it is.' She pours the drink. But as she does so she then deliberately emits a noticeable whimper. She says, 'Oh dear, that's the last bottle. We're out of vodka for the rest of this flight.'

Hats off to her. This is perhaps the finest example of damage limitation that I will witness throughout the whole tour.

*

A few of the group get rowdy, Bonehead in particular. Nothing extreme, just raised voices. But Noel checks it. He asks the worried attendant for pen and paper. Then, with a huge grin on his face, he walks down the aisle asking all the other passengers to sign a petition. 'It's to have Oasis banned from Air France,' he explains.

'I don't know about you, mate,' he confidentially tells one man as he hands over the pen, 'but I can't bleeding stand them. Or their music.' Some of the passengers sign the paper, look amused. But most pointedly ignore the smiling songwriter.

*

By the time we get to Barcelona, Bonehead is beyond. The world spins in front of him like a revolving mirror ball. We come through customs, pushing trolleys. Bonehead grabs one for support. But his legs aren't up to it. They give way. He falls heavily but manages to grab the leg of the trolley. He screams, 'Aggghhh!' and so makes his entrance into the crowded airport, being dragged across the floor. A gaggle of Spanish reporters are waiting for the band. They spot Noel and make a bee-line for him, surrounding him with cameras.

Liam and Terry come up from behind, do neat body swerves and avoid the scrum that is developing. As Noel is surrounded by cameras and questions, Bonehead now arrives, still being dragged along the floor.

Noel sees him and instantly turns and pretends to stomp on his guitarist as he slides on by. Cameras flash and all the time the words 'Lightweight!' and 'Geezer!' are reverberating around the airport.

Finally the band and crew make it to the van that is waiting and climb aboard. But Bonehead isn't finished. Not by a long chalk. As the reporters and cameras surround the van, Bonehead shouts, 'You want it, do ya? Well, cop for this, you cunts.' Then he pulls down his strides and fully exposes his buttocks to the entire Spanish media. 'Come on!' he cries again. 'Who wants it?' And the van moves off.

*

The next night. Restaurant. We gather in the lobby below. Liam sits on a small desk talking cordially with a fan. The mood is good.

A hotel security guard spots Liam, approaches and then pokes him in the ribs. Tells him to get off the desk. Bad move. Not clever. Not with his temperament. Instantly riled, Liam turns on him, furiously tells the guard, Hey, hey, hey, you want me to move then ask nicely and I'll fucking move. But don't you go poking me in the ribs because I'll fucking do you, you cunt. The security guard takes this in, turns on his feet and immediately seeks out the hotel manager, who smiles briefly when told of the incident. It's the opening he's been looking for. He has little time for Oasis. A bunch of pissed-up Mancs with a rep for drink, damage and drugs running loose in his vast and brand-new modernistic hotel? Hardly the kind of clientele he wishes to attract.

In fact, the manager wants nothing more than to be rid of these turbulent musicians. So he gives the order, the curt order that Maggie is dreading. Kick them out. Now. Take their bags out of their rooms and put them out with the cats. Where they belong. So now Maggie has to go and calm the waters, convince him that it was all a misunderstanding. Finally he very reluctantly agrees that the group can stay. He just can't believe that the last time he saw one of the band was on the national news. And he had his buttocks bared to the camera.

*

Guigsy saw it on TV as well, but Noel didn't. After checking into the hotel Noel was due to be driven to a radio station for a live interview. But then a message speedily arrived. Please don't bother, it said. Stay at the hotel. 'But I'm up for it,' cried Noel.

'We're not,' they replied. They too had watched the news and seen the rotten state of Noel Gallagher. If the rhythm guitarist was baring all, imagine what the song-writer would do.

'When I woke up this morning,' Bonehead announced at the restaurant, 'I thought, Oh no, what have I done? Then I was in the shower and I just started laughing my tits off.'

'The thing is, though, Bone,' Guigsy said, hardly able to contain his glee, 'it wasn't just your harris that was on view. The way it was shot, you could actually see your balls dangling between your legs.'

'No!'

'I'm telling you straight. Last night your balls were seen by millions of Spanish people. And when that picture gets back to England and is plastered all over the front pages of all the newspapers, you are going to be right in the shit.'

'No, I'm not. Kate will be fine about it. But shit! Her mother! Oh, fuck. Can you imagine Christmas Day? All of us seated around the table, big turkey and all that and the mother shaking her head, thinking, I've seen my son-in-law's bollocks. Oh no.'

Bonehead buried his head in his hands and Liam raised his glass. ''E' are, everybody. This band has done loads of mad things. Fucking drinking too much, hotels wrecked, dodgy birds, all the drugs and that. But never – EVER – has one of us showed his balls on national TV. Come on, the Bonehead!'

*

At the gig, in Zaragoza's Pabellón Principe Felipe, Gareth (the onstage monitor man) told Carole (the sound technician), 'Tell Liam not to smash the mikes tonight. There's only two of the fuckers left.' At this juncture in the tour Liam had demolished about 20 microphones. Maybe that was why the first half of the show was perhaps the best I have ever heard Liam sing. Most gigs, Liam had come over so threatening, smashed his fist into the mike so many times, that people backed away from the band. But tonight his actions were severely limited. He could only sing. And sing he did, for he was magnificent.

Raw, powerful, urgent, sneering Liam, he mixed soul with rock'n'roll and did what every musician sets out to do every night but knows only happens fitfully; and that is not put a foot wrong and fully communicate with the audience. Liam was big time, full throttle. Coupled with the band's potency, it was music that opened up your head and allowed the spirit to enter your body. Exhilarating.

'Like an angel,' is how Bonehead's wife Kate first described Liam when he auditioned for the band at Bonehead's house and she sat in the bath and listened to him for the very first time. Same thing here, an avenging angel in full control. In fact, the first half of the show, until the pace slackened, was reminiscent of that rapturous show in Aberdeen. I wasn't the only one who thought so.

In the dressing room afterwards, Ocean Colour Scene's vocalist, Simon Fowler, enthused, 'Fuck, that restored my love for rock'n'roll. They're so much better when the pressure's off them. Look at Liam. He just doesn't look old any more.'

And it was true. Away from the boiler-house pressure that is England, the band could relax a little. Here the press were not as intrusive and the fans less demanding.

Meanwhile a buoyant Liam was saying, 'My family say to me [adopts Irish accent], "Bejesus, that Bonehead, he's a fine fellow." I go, What are you on about? He's a top pisshead. Then they say, "Ah, that Guigsy, such a nice man." Yeah and he's a top pothead. "Ah, but that Alan White." Yeah and he's a top pervert. My family all think you're great except for me and my kid, who apparently are crackhead, coke-sniffing hooligans.'

*

At the airport, Noel sat against a wall reading an Elvis book, the one written by his entourage, the famed Memphis Mafia. Suddenly Noel exclaimed, 'Check this out.' He started reading out aloud: '"Something is bound to happen when you put Elvis, eight geezers, a chimpanzee and 152 women together in a house."'

Noel set the book aside. 'Jesus,' he purred admiringly, 'no wonder they called him The King. A chimpanzee! How top is that?'

*

In the dressing room of Barcelona's Palais des Sports, everyone is present apart from Liam. There are ten minutes to go before showtime. Unlike the dressing rooms we have encountered – normally huge rooms with mirrors and bright lights and tables full of fruit and snacks and booze – this one is small and homely. The band sit. They are silent and impatient. Finally Noel breaks the silence.

Noel: What are those?

Mike Rowe: Cigarette papers with messages from fans on them.

Noel: Really?

Mike: Yep. This one is from Sonia.

Noel (shaking his head): Nah. No good. Never trust a girl called Sonia.

Mike: Why not?

Noel: Because they've always got one eye, no teeth and a kid.

Paul Stacey: Sounds like my girlfriend.

Noel (settling back): This chair is so comfy. Think I'll nick it and put it in my house.

He closes his eyes. More silence. Everyone sits motionless and stares at the faded red carpet, the dull wallpaper. No movement, nothing. Another eternal minute passes.

Eventually Bonehead stands up, paces around. Paul, Mike and Guigsy do likewise. They flex their arms, crack knuckles, let out big sighs. Their movements disturb Noel, who now opens his eyes.

'We off?' he asks hopefully.

'Nah, not yet,' says Bonehead.

Through the walls the faint thud of Phil Smith's records can be heard. That is the only noise. Everyone now sits down. No one looks at each other. The tension is palpable until the door opens and in walks Liam. He claps his hands together. 'Shall we have a laugh and a joke tonight?'

'A laugh and a joke?' Guigsy quizzically asks.

'That's right, man,' Liam replies.

'What's a laugh and a joke onstage like?'

'Some nights it's like . . .' – Liam mimics a guitarist, wired and violently thrashing his instrument – 'and other nights it's . . . a laugh and a joke.'

Liam sits down. Silence descends. Now Liam starts clapping his hands. Then the door opens again. Everyone looks up expectantly, like children waiting for the birthday cake. It's Maggie, holding a torch. 'It's time,' she says.

'Thank fuck for that,' Noel says.

'Come on then,' Liam shouts. 'Let's kill them.'

And Oasis saunter out to meet that night's destiny.

*

Liam and I stay up till about six or seven in room 222 of the Meridien Hotel, Barcelona. We drink, we talk and then we shout for more. I have notes from that conversation but they tell me nothing. They are the scribbles that dare to be understood. I remember we spoke about James, Patsy's son, for whom Liam would catch ten kinds of bullets and then some. (In fact, I do have one readable note which says that, although Liam is smart, sharp, funny, blah blah blah, there's a place inside he'll never let you into. So maybe, just maybe, out of all the people walking this earth, it is a five-year-old kid who can claim to know Liam best.)

I remember we went into how Oasis are portrayed by the media – one-dimensional – and Liam admitted to playing up to the press because they were all dicks who wouldn't understand him or the band in a million years, so why not dick them around?

I recall a discussion about how Oasis affected people, what the band meant to so many people, including its own members. Like Liam. But the only quote I can run with that I know for sure emanated from Liam's mouth was this: 'I wish people would realize just how funny the people in this fucking band is.'

And then the morning crawled in on all fours and begged us to let it get on with its magic. So we parted and crawled into our own dreams.

And the next day Paul Weller was arrested.

*

'It was probably for being a 40-year-old Mod,' Liam sniggered.

It was about four in the afternoon when the story came through. We were leaving Spain for Switzerland, Geneva to be precise, and most of us were huddled with our hangovers around coffees. The news of Weller's arrest in Paris for hotel damage beyond the call of duty had been faxed through to Noel.

'All I have to do,' he announced, 'is close my eyes and I can see him right now, walking round in circles in that cell, kicking the walls, going, "Cunts! Cunts!"'

Then he ordered pen and paper, drew a picture of Weller in a stripy prisoner's uniform, added the word 'lightweight!' next to it, signed it from everyone and had it faxed through to his incarcerated friend who had spent the night cooling off in a Parisian cell.

*

Arrival, Geneva time, was about ten o'clock that night. There was a small white Transit van waiting for us. We crowded in. Liam was tired, hungover and not impressed by the transport. Not at all. 'International rock stars and look at us. In a Transit van. A fucking Paddy band, that's what we are.' He sat down, bad head upon him.

'We need Coyley sat right here,' Noel said, pointing at the driver's seat and thinking – once more – of the fun-filled old days when life was a gas because no one gave a shit and there weren't thousands of people you had to play for and take seriously.

'Fuck off,' Bonehead said, 'it was me doing all the driving.'

Noel ignored him, carried on reminiscing. 'We need Coyley going, Where are we going? How do we get there? Remember that time in Liverpool when the cops stopped us and opened up the back door. Smoke billowing out of the van, all of us pissed as cunts. They took one look and said, Nah, too much trouble this, we'll leave it.' Noel sat back and stared out of the window. Keeping him company was a mind replaying a past that was threatening to be a lot more fun than the future.

*

This is how close the friendships run. At about 12.30 that night I hear a noise outside my room and go to investigate. It's Guigsy, who's dropped his keys.

'Where you off to, boss?'

'Well, I was going to chill in my room but I'm going down to see Liam because he's charged up and he's on his own down there and there is bound to be someone there who doesn't know the score. But if he sees me that will chill him out and he'll be as sweet as.'

As sweet as.

*

For this part of the tour, The Seahorses took over support slot. Onstage in Geneva, John Squire, their guitarist and leader, asked, 'Who's the cunt with all the Nazi gold then?'

*

After the show, which wasn't the best ever, Liam looked round the dressing room and announced, 'I can't wait for us to grow 'taches, shorten our trousers and become crackheads.'

*

Everyone was now calling Noel 'the Chief'. 'Chief around, is he?' 'How's the Chief?' 'What mood is the Chief in?' 'Is the Chief all right?'

Big Chief, Little Chief. I didn't say nish – you don't on tour – but this Chief business, it was really starting to grate. Or, put another way, touring was perfect for Noel to pull rank.

Here on the road, there was an unspoken rule that you never upset the equilibrium. Example? You don't like this person? Cool. But you sort it out at home. The gig, the band, these come first in your life. Get used to it.

That was ground rule one. The second was: don't piss off the man who brought you here. And this is where Noel took advantage. He saw how everyone was so careful to tread softly around him. Chief this, Chief that. Got you this, Chief, got you that. Noel basked in our absolute acquiescence to him.

He made sure that everyone knew he was top dog. If he found himself losing an argument his face would turn to a sneer and he would snap, 'Don't forget, you work for me, mate.' That usually did it. I had been on other Oasis tours where Noel used similar language, but it had always been delivered with tongue in cheek. But on this tour, the humour was markedly absent.

Maybe it was because he took too much on his plate, insisting that he be consulted on every aspect of the band.

Maybe it was because Oasis were now what he never envisaged them to be: a huge money-making machine that was forced to place professionalism above everything else. Maybe it was because he was no longer considered *numero uno* songwriter. Maybe it was because the critical sniping had finally got to him. Seven months working on an album and these students were calling it a turkey?

Or maybe it was everything with a dash of pure-ego-tripping poured on for good measure. In Miles Davis's autobiography the trumpeter has just bought a hew Lamborghini and he's taken it for a spin. He's stopped by the police. He's doing 125 miles an hour.

'Sir,' says the officer. 'Why were you doing 125 miles an hour?'

Miles answered, 'Look at this car. Wouldn't you?'

I think Noel looked at us all – Chief this, Chief that – and said, wouldn't you?

*

John Squire is onstage in Bologna, Italy. 'That Mussolini was a bit of a cunt,' he tells the audience.

*

All day the knives had been out. Italy versus Russia. Winner qualifies for the World Cup. I didn't watch the show that night. Stayed in the dressing room with Squire and watched Italy qualify. If they hadn't I may well have caught the first plane home. I'm serious. Rather that than face this army of piss-takers.

*

We catch the train to Milan. After the show, Noel was in a happy mood but Liam still seemed restrained, distracted. The gig had been held in a huge complex on the outskirts of town. Outside there were at least 50 stalls selling bootleg Oasis stuff. T-shirts, mainly.

It had been a strange show. Part of the crowd seemed in awe. The rest kept their own counsel and posed hard. They like being snobs in this part of Italy. In Milan it is crucial that you hold onto your cool. Nothing dislodges it. Not even fierce rock'n'roll.

Danny, the bodyguard, entered the room, told us that there was an after-show party. Noel wasn't interested but the rest of us – apart from Liam – went to check out the party. About half an hour later I went back to get some drinks out of the dressing room. I could hear Slade's 'How Does It Feel?' blaring out and could see Terry barring entrance to the room.

'Liam's in there,' he explained, 'he wants to be left alone.'

'Cool.'

*

On the bus on the way home, Guigsy sat next to Liam. I don't know what was troubling the man but I saw the bassist fling a protective arm around the singer and I heard Liam quietly say, 'I don't like Liam Gallagher at the moment.' Touring does that to you.

*

This hotel – Milan's Four Seasons – was perhaps the plushest we would stay in on this leg of the tour. The rooms were opulent, grand. You felt rich just sitting in here. And that was just my little cubby-hole. Fuck knows what the band's were like. They stayed in the suites. At the bar downstairs, Liam, still quiet, distracted, had a quick drink and then disappeared. I stayed for a few more and then decided bedways was bestways. As I approached reception I now saw Danny standing there watching Bonehead argue with the manager.

'Someone should do something,' I heard the guitarist angrily complain. 'There's stuff everywhere. It stinks. I'm not going to my room when it's like that. Now you clean it up and if you don't find out who let off that fire extinguisher then I'm going to make sure you're held responsible.'

'What's going on?' I ask.

Danny now turns to me. 'Just leave it,' he says. But he does so in his this-is-a-blag-so-don't-fuck-it-up voice.

'It's outrageous,' Bonehead complained. 'People letting off fire extinguishers. The corridor where my room is stinks and it's gone in all the carpets.'

Just as the manager is about to speak there is a commotion by the front door. A giggling bunch of young Italian girls, fresh from the concert, burst into the hotel.

The manager's face turns red. 'No, no, please, they can't come in,' he cries as they rush by him.

''E' are, mate,' Bonehead says, trying to regain the manager's attention but all the time sensing his plan to double-bluff him is about to fail. 'Don't worry about them, let's get this extinguisher business sorted first.'

The manager totally ignores him. He fumbles for the phone as the girls head to the bar. Sweat is now breaking out on his forehead. He is a moment away from cracking. Then he makes his decision. He wants Oasis out of the hotel. Now.

Rob and Terry spent most of the night calming the guy down, persuading him that it was not such a good idea to call the cops. After all, the girls had been rounded up before they could get to the lifts and they had been ejected. As for the fire extinguisher, could they prove for certain, as Liam Gallagher drank beer in a room on the third floor, that it was the singer who had let off the fire extinguisher, so causing the entire air conditioning system to be shut down? (The foam had fatefully been sucked into the system.)

Actually, they could. It would all be on camera.

OK, but we're going tomorrow, so can't you just let us stay a few more hours and then we'll be gone for good. Promise.

The bill came to thousands of pounds. Many thousands. The Four Seasons management were an inch away from banning Oasis from every one of their hotels world-wide.

At ten that morning Noel Gallagher was in an excellent mood. 'Lucky you fuckers didn't wake me up,' he said, surveying the red-eyed posse before him. 'As it was, I had a top kip, woke up, saw some white stuff on the floor and thought, Where the fuck were you when I needed you last night?'

*

On Wednesday 19 November, as the band played a good gig in Munich, Spurs lost to Crystal Palace and plunged even further towards relegation. The entire crew and band laughed at me. And then we went to Prague.

*

At the airport, young guys in uniforms ushered us into a waiting room while Immigration dealt with passports and visas. Noel was in a good mood. Meg would be waiting for him at the hotel. We would not see him until the next night's gig. As usual he, Strangeboy and Mike Rowe were talking instruments.

'Have you seen that 1967 Epiphone guitar I've got?' Noel asked them. 'Got it off this guy in Birmingham. I was in his shop and he was showing me all the guitars and I said, "What's out back?" And he started getting all shifty, going, "Nah, nothing out there, mate". I thought, You little fucker. So I went back and saw this beautiful 1967 Epiphone.

'He said to me, "Oh, man, I've been saving up 18 months for that."'

'I said, "Come on, give it over." And that's how I got it.'

Which was nice. For Noel.

*

Prague is cold, bitterly so. The black-winged wind whips through the streets, passing easily through the city's numerous Gothic-style buildings.

Havel, the country's poetic, heroic Prime Minister, is seriously ill and the subsequent gloom seems to have seeped from his palace bedroom into the city. But Oasis are in town. Not many bands pass this way. There is a touch of expectation in the air. Music put it there. And the people, buttoned up against the cold by coats and smiles, move around the town squares, buying and selling, buying and selling.

The *NME* are here to photograph the band for their Christmas issue. But they don't take pictures of Oasis out in the street. They mock up a room and shoot them there. And all the people on the tour say, strange.

The band play Prague's cavernous Sporthall. Seventeen thousand people are in for the show, and they can hardly contain themselves when Oasis hit the stage. I stand next to John Squire as Liam announces, "This is called "D'You Know What I Mean?" and I fucking hope someone does.'

'So underrated this song,' I tell Squire.

'It's my fave as well. That and "Live Forever".'

'Do you think Noel has got better as a guitarist?' I ask him.

'Definitely, but the funny thing is, when you walk out onstage you forget everything you've ever learnt. It just goes and you think, Fucking hell, what am I doing here? That's why you can find yourself onstage. Look at Liam.'

We both glance over at Gallagher Junior, who is bouncing up and down onstage. 'See what I mean?' Squire says with a relaxed smile.

Most of the band go out that night, local bars and clubs. But there is little action, nothing major to report. Oasis have played and Prague people go back to their lives, back to the cold, back to their buying and selling.

It had been a bad week for personalities. On Tuesday Gary Glitter was pulled in for questioning by the police. On Friday a vicious rumour that Paul Weller had died swept Fleet Street. And on Saturday, as Oasis brought their message of personal freedom to 17,000 Czechs, Michael Hutchence committed suicide. 'I'd better keep my head down,' Noel said in the hotel lobby.

*

We were due to drive from Prague to Berlin, but the fog was so intense that train travel was deemed easier. Noel and Meg decided to chance it by road.

We drive to the station and meet up with The Seahorses. I sit with Marcus Russell and Steve Adge, The Seahorses' tour manager. Adge once worked with The Stone Roses, helped put on their early legendary gigs. He's something of a face around Manchester. Everyone knows The Adge. He is stocky, bearded, seemingly always cheerful. Marcus, by contrast, is clean-shaven, given to wearing cords and bulky sweaters. Although he cites Peter Grant, Led Zeppelin's boisterous manager, as a role model, Marcus is not flamboyant in any way. He prefers to work behind the scenes, away from the lights.

Adge now asked Marcus if the band had been keen to tour.

'Well, after the album was completed,' Marcus replied, 'I didn't say a word. It wasn't me saying, Right, this is what we're doing. That approach would have been totally wrong. The only downside is that everywhere we play we're late in terms of how long the album has been out.'

'Are you selling out everywhere?' Steve enquired.

'The UK, fine. Outside of there, we have to work at it. Which is really good.'

'Why?'

'Because,' Marcus emphasized, 'it keeps us in the real world.'

*

Liam entered the carriage with his fourth lager of the day in hand. Most of the knuckles on his right hand were bruised or cut from punching mikes. It was midday, Sunday 23 November, and the spirit was upon him.

'I have met the Devil,' he announced. 'I even made him a cup of tea and then I said, Right, you great big fat truck driver, get the fuck out of here.'

'What are you talking about?' Marcus gently asked, strains of his Welsh accent notably surfacing.

'The Devil, man, the Devil. Right? See, you can say my stuff is crap. Or God, please save me. Right? But, I'm telling you, man, no one will. You have to do it all yourself. Patsy's into it but I'm not. I don't believe in God or the Devil. Right?'

When Liam preached like this, he would always end each sentence with the last word framed as a question before intently glaring at you for confirmation. 'All you need is respect, patience and loyalty. Right?'

'Is that all you need?' Marcus said with a slight chuckle.

Liam ignored him. Carried on. 'So I made the Devil a cup of tea and told him to leave. Do you know what he said?'

'No. What?'

'Give us some more milk.'

Liam stood up and exited. There was a brief silence and then Steve Adge said, 'Just like Ian Brown. Just the same.'

'The exact same thing?' I enquired, intrigued by the comparison. Liam would have been the first to acknowledge that he lifted some of Brown's stage persona. But I was unaware that both characters were cut from the same cloth.

'Yeah, except with Ian it wasn't as funny,' Adge sighed. 'I'm not joking. Sometimes we'd tape Ian and then at three in the morning find some deserted castle, sit him down and say, Now listen to the shit you come out with.'

The carriage door flew open and Liam stepped back in. Round two.

'I've just asked these kids from England out there what the word is on Oasis. Not fucking press or that shit. But you know what people on the street think. Know what they said? Oasis only travel with West Ham firms.' This was a reference to the band's security guards, who all hailed – apart from Rob – from London.

An amused expression may have crossed Liam's drunken face when he heard this but now the aggression was taking over.

'Fucking right we're seen with a West Ham firm, fucking right,' he shouted. 'They come home with me. See, they're talking about the Manchester gig that's coming up. Remember that kidnap threat bullshit I had?' [Whenever Oasis play their hometown dark threats from all parts of Manchester rain down on them.]

'Well, I'm arsed. When we play Manchester do you know exactly what I'm going to do? I'm going to see my mum and I'm going to visit my Auntie Helen. Then I'm going to go to the alleyway where I lost my cherry and then I'm going to walk up and down Market Street ten times. And then I'm going to play some music for the kids who want to hear it. Then I'm going to go home and when I do go home it is going to be with a bunch of West Ham hooligans.'

And with that, Liam left the carriage. To sit with West Ham people. Deliberately.

That night, on the coach to the Berlin gig – The Messehalle 2, capacity 14,350, sold out, good going – Liam was still pissed, belligerent. He insisted on playing through the coach's music system the two b-sides Oasis had recently recorded. And he insisted on playing them so loud that the music simply distorted into a maelstrom of fuzz and feedback. Painful to say the least. But not one of us complained.

*

At the gig the first thing the drunk Liam did was to walk into the arena and straight up to the barriers separating audience from the band and stand there, arms outstretched. Within seconds, excited fans were crowding round him, shouting his name, demanding his signature. Terry, Liam's man, came rushing by. 'I could slap him sometimes,' he muttered, 'but I can't help loving him.'

*

Noel had arrived by now. He had already been interviewed by the *NME* for their Christmas edition.

'What did you say to your detractors?' I asked him.

'That however much those *NME* writers hate us we will always hate them even more.'

Fighting stuff. But he sounded defensive.

*

Liam was well on the way now, the belligerence really starting to seep through. Noel smelt it first and the brothers had words. Nothing too major but enough for Noel to tell Meg before the gig, 'I think it might be best if we shoot off straight away. I'm not hanging around with him like that.'

Liam onstage: 'Forgive me, forgive me, I can't reach the high notes.' Given his inebriation, this was not a major revelation.

*

Straight after the gig, I stood by the mixing desk and Huw said to me, 'What did you think of that?'

'Shit. Not as bad as Sheffield, but shit.'

Later, in the dressing room, Bonehead asked Huw, 'What did you think of the gig?'

'Terrible,' Huw replied.

'You're fucking joking,' Bonehead immediately replied. 'That was fucking top.'

'No. It wasn't good. Believe me.'

Huw sipped on his beer. He, like so many of the Oasis road crew, defied the roadie stereotype. His clothes were casual but not dirty, sweaty. He was well-read, professional and skilled, as they all had to be now, in new technology. He also had about three months left in his job. Soon he would walk.

'Go easy on Huw,' Guigsy told Bonehead after Huw had left the room. 'His dad's in a bad way.'

'Well, he should go home,' snapped Bonehead, still smarting from the criticism. 'No point in playing the fucking hero. Me, I'd be off like a shot.'

And me, I kept quiet.

*

The next night, in my Hanover hotel room, I make a call. 'Hello, it's me.'

'Hi. How you doing?'

'Not bad. Shows have been good. Couple of shit ones but overall everything is top. What's been happening back home?'

'You sound like you've got a hangover.'

'No, I'm in Hanover.'

'Bit of a drink then?'

'No, no. Very quiet last night.'

'Really?'

'Yeah.'

'Are you sure?'

'Look, nothing happened. Strangeboy didn't get accidentally headbutted on the nose and smacked in the mouth by Noel and Bonehead. And Noel certainly didn't drop his trousers. No one went running through the hotel shouting their mouths off. No one approached two German residents in the hotel bar with a couple of drinks and said, "Oi, cunty bollocks, get these down your neck."

'It certainly wasn't Alan White taking over the bar and dishing out drinks to everyone like that character Dave in *Minder* and doing so to spontaneous eruptions of "Geezer! Geezer!" from the assembled. And there certainly wasn't anybody wearing two cowboy hats, an orange wool hat on top of them, complete with sunglasses, calling themselves the nine-stone cowboy. It's also totally untrue that a security guard took out his third leg and dipped it in a pint of lager.'

'Good drink then.'

'Very good drink.'

*

A day later, after two credible shows in Hanover and Frankfurt, we made our way to Frankfurt Airport. The photographer Jill Furmanovsky had now joined us for a brief spell.

Noel wore a cowboy hat and shades. He was drunk but still going, having been up all night with Strangeboy and Mike Rowe.

At the airport, as Maggie collected tickets, Noel opened his guitar case, sat cross-legged on the floor and started playing 'He's Got The Whole World In His Hands', to the bemusement of the passengers present. Then he posed with the rest of the band for Jill's camera. Then he poured himself on the plane. I sat next to him. Immediately, he started talking about the next Oasis album. This one, he revealed, would be written and recorded and then handed over to a variety of remixers such as The Chemical Brothers.

'Won't having all those people remixing the songs make the album sound disjointed?' I asked.

Noel looked at me like I was stupid. 'Exactly,' he said. Then he ordered another drink.

And the plane dipped towards Holland.

*

At the hotel bar in Amsterdam I sat with a slowly sinking Noel and sober Jill Furmanovsky. She told us that just before her arrival Creation Records had called and requested she not supply *Mojo* with any more photos of Oasis.

The source of the problem was a recent front-cover article on the band. The writer was Nick Kent, the man who had shot the Oasis documentary for Canal+. He had tried to sell his film to British TV but the band's management had stopped him. Instead, he transcribed all the interviews, passed them on to *Mojo*. The magazine's front-page headline screamed: 'BANNED! The documentary they didn't want you to see.' Noel was not amused. Nor were Creation. Hence their request to Jill.

'But I, as a freelance photographer, can't do that,' she explained, 'because that's my living. *Mojo* are clients of mine. I don't want to piss them off.'

Noel was sympathetic to her plight. "That's the trouble with the band these days,' he mooted. 'Everyone is taking everything far too seriously. Gets right on my tits.' Then he raised his glass. 'Fuck it, let's get large.'

And at five o'clock the next morning Rob the security guard picked up a semi-unconscious Noel in a bar and carried him back to his hotel. 'Time to go home, Chief,' he cheerfully announced, slinging the songwriter over his back.

*

The final show of Oasis's European tour took place on 28 November in The Arena, Oberhausen. Noel and Liam's voices were both shot through. Their singing was off-key, off time. Subsequently the band struggled through the set. It was painful, but that was it. Second leg over.

And then, on the bus home, Noel found out that the gig had been recorded for transmission on German national radio the very next day.

'No fucking way,' he shouted. 'Rob, you get that tape and then I'll fucking burn it.'

He turned and stared moodily out of the window at the blackened scenery. There was silence. Then he turned back towards us and, with that smile of his, said, 'Actually, why don't we offer all the listeners a tape of the show and then put a sticker on it saying, "Burn Here Now"?'

Everyone laughed and the next night we slept in our own beds.

THREE

HOME FROM HOME
Dublin to Manchester

True or false?
'Those who break down the doors are destined to be trampled on by those coming in behind them.'

Paolo Hewitt, Christmas '97

FOR Oasis, Dublin might as well have been home ground, home turf. The people here loved them with a passion that often overstepped the borders of mania. The Gallaghers. Oasis. Their own and of their own. Fucking deadly. And irresistible.

Look at how they shouted their mouths off but then screwed everyone because they backed it up with enormous talent. Look at how they had pulled themselves up by their bootlaces and beaten the world. The Irish admired that kind of spirit. Many of them were well versed in what it took to leave the gutter behind.

Noel and Liam. Gallaghers. Irish. Ours. (Even if the crafty buggers did support England at football. Which was very Irish.)

It was six-thirty p.m. and Noel – dressed in jeans, leather jacket – and Mike Rowe were sat in the dressing room of The Point – the scene of one of the greatest-ever Oasis gigs, the Morning Glory tour 1995 – when Marcus walked in, wanting to look at the future.

South America was first on the agenda.

'Now I need to know if you want to go there or not because there's still time to put it together,' he explained, setting down his briefcase, pulling off his coat. This dressing room was small, intimate. Like someone's front room. The chairs were old, comfy. The sofa well worn. Domesticity beckoned in this room.

Marcus's manner was brisk, business-like. He had been with the band for years now, knew them well. He suited them. One of his real strengths was his refusal to panic, a vital quality to possess when dealing with Oasis and the chaos they liked to cause everywhere.

'Now can I explain how I see it and then you tell me what you think?' Marcus asked Noel. And before the songwriter could answer, he continued, 'See, what I thought was the best thing to do would be to return from the Australian tour, have a week off, charge up the batteries, all that kind of thing. Then on to Paris for the cancelled show and throw in a Hamburg as well. I mean, it's ridiculous we didn't play there. It's a huge town for us.'

'So why didn't we play there?' Noel asked. He had his surly head on today, could hear it in his voice.

'They said they couldn't get the right venue,' Marcus quickly explained. 'Anyway from there I reckon a quick Belgium date and then on to Mexico. How do you feel about that?'

Noel looked at his manager with a bored, almost contemptuous look.

'Can't say fairer than that, I suppose,' Marcus replied with a short grin. 'I'll take that as a yes then.'

The talk now moved on to a proposed new single, something to follow the forthcoming 'All Around The World'.

Oasis had already agreed to shift its release date away from Christmas. Everyone agreed. No point in competing with The Spice Girls. No point, either, in slagging them off. Marcus suggested 'Don't Go Away', but Noel said he preferred the album's title track. Marcus disagreed. Softly. '"Don't Go Away" will get more radio play,' he explained.

'When's it due for?' Noel asked.

'Well, 6 April is the first possible date.'

'But that means I'll have to write some b-sides,' Noel protested. 'And I'll have to do that over Christmas and to be quite honest with you I want to develop a serious drug habit this Christmas.' He turned to Mike Rowe and said, 'I write some of my best problems on drugs.'

'Problems,' Rowe cried. 'You said "problems". I say, what a Freudian slip.'

'No,' Noel said, recovering smartly, 'I said I write some of my best drugs on songs.'

*

The Dublin gig was the equivalent of an open goal. After their previous shows here, the band knew just how much they meant in this neck of the world. Such was their determination to repeat those triumphs, even Liam deigned to make the soundcheck.

But that night, despite the audience's full-on reaction and unequivocal demonstration of love, the band walked off dispirited, dejected. Onstage the sound had been horrific. They couldn't hear each other, they couldn't lock into each other, and that meant they couldn't give these people the proper Oasis, the Oasis of Aberdeen and Spain. The Oasis of Dublin two years ago. Frustration.

In the dressing room it was as if a sickening piece of news had just been delivered. Tension hovered above everyone's heads as they sat slumped in chairs, staring at the floor, staring at nothing. The very next day Meg arrived.

*

As soon as she walked in, saw Noel unable to sit still, she knew something was up.

'Are you all right, love?'

'I would be if I had a fucking singer.'

'Liam hasn't shown up for the soundcheck?' Meg asked, putting down her bag.

'No. Liam's not singing tonight.'

'Why? What's the problem?'

'I don't know, I don't know.' Noel stopped pacing around the room. He sat down in a nearby chair and started chewing on his nails. Then staring at them. Hard. Meg waited for Noel. She knew him so well now.

'There's something up with his throat,' he finally explained.

'Well, has he seen a doctor?'

The answer better be yes. The group needed a certificate for insurance purposes. Ward off potential loss of money. In fact, protect a lot of moolah from disappearing out of the Oasis account. The answer *was* yes. Liam had nodules on his throat. The doctor had advised several weeks' rest. Impossible. There were still dates in Glasgow, Cardiff, Manchester and London to complete before Christmas forced them off the road.

Liam was now consigned to bed and prescribed a series of steroids. For the time being Noel would have to undertake all vocal duties. Consequently signs were put up by the door announcing that a refund for the show was available.

Twenty people out of 8000 asked for their money back and Oasis, backs to the wall, turned in one of the best shows of the tour.

It was the band's determination, a source that was first located in Noel and then brutally translated to the others, that swung it. Here's a challenge. Liam's missing. I'll sing. Now. You up for it? Or what?

Whatever you say, Chief.

Then the master-stroke. The reintroduction of Noel's acoustic set. A far better show now emerged. For here, with guitar and solitary spotlight for company, singing songs such as 'Stand By Me' and 'Don't Go Away', Noel brought Oasis back to the people. This is what had been missing, that sense of community, that us-against-them vibe, that this band had summoned up so often and so effortlessly in the past.

And although the original set list was invigorating – how could it not be with songs such as 'Champagne Supernova' or 'D'You Know What I Mean?', 'Live Forever' – I realized now that in part it obscured the quality of songs, allowed Oasis the option to bludgeon their audience into submission.

They were concentrating too much on upping the energy levels when they should have been colouring in the cracks. The acoustic guitar section gave the set valuable light and shade. And even though it would not be reintroduced until America, the seeds had been sown.

It was a cracking night. The audience willed Oasis to greater heights and Noel responded with a display of guitar playing and singing that all who witnessed it will remember for a long, long time. He took that audience and he shook them hard. Left them breathless, cheering. He was everything he ever said he was.

Afterwards, in the dressing room, it was as if the FA Cup had been won. Now there were smiles and jokes and piss-takes. Celebrate the night, have a good time. But all too quickly Noel got off quick with Meg and the rest of us retired to the hotel, suddenly a little subdued.

And then the very next day Liam threatened to kick my face in.

*

It started in the hotel at about three in the afternoon. Sipping on his Guinness in the hotel bar, Liam looked refreshed after his night's rest. His mood was benign. He joked with the other band members (apart from Noel, who had opted to stay elsewhere with Meg), told them playfully not to get too used to him being offstage. Bonehead told him that Noel had changed the set around, introduced 'Cigarettes And Alcohol', and they hadn't played it for so long it had thrown them.

'Fucking glad I'm not singing tonight,' Liam joked. 'I couldn't remember any of those songs either.'

Then Liam wondered out loud if he should come to the gig. Terry advised him against it. 'Look at it from the fan's point of view,' he reasoned. 'They're told that you're ill. Then they show up at the gig and there you are. It's not going to make much sense to them, is it? You can hardly stand there and tell each one of them that it's your throat which is fucked but the rest of you is fine. Can you?'

'Yeah, I know what you're saying,' Liam replied. But a shadow of doubt passed noticeably over his brooding face.

*

Mouse got it first. She was the cook that Oasis insisted on employing for every UK tour. Mouse was a skilled professional, a cheery indomitable woman who oversaw the provision of three meals a day for over 50 people.

She was also a firm believer in matters spiritual. Every day, before work, she would write her Thought For The Day on a blackboard and place it in a prominent position. (One day Noel strolled in and, seeing the blackboard blank, wrote on it: 'Nobody Is Good At Everything But Everyone Is Good At Something'.)

When Liam walked into her kitchen, Mouse was surprised to see him. She didn't know that the singer had been taking steroids and then pouring alcohol on top of them. She didn't know that at some point after our departure Liam had got it into his head that no one wanted him at the gig and that the lethal mix inside him was now raising his paranoia to extremely dangerous levels.

She didn't know all that. She just knew that she was surprised to see Liam, and she told him so. And the next thing she knows Liam has blown up in her face. Who the fuck was she to tell him how to behave? He'd do what he fucking liked. It was his gig, his band. And who the fuck was she?

Mouse fought back. Liam fought back. Mouse waved her finger at him and Liam told her never to do that. Or what? Mouse replied. They stood in the kitchen and hurled insults, bad insults, until Liam finally turned and walked away. Towards me.

*

Travis were the new support group. Most of Oasis would watch them every night. Not because pre-gig time was so boring that anything to kill it was welcomed with open arms, but because Travis had songs such as 'More Than Us' and 'All I Wanna Do Is Rock' and they were talented and their enthusiasm for the work infectious. Noel and I were side-stage checking them when Liam appeared. His first words, delivered in a voice of fury and demand, were: 'Is it all right for me to stand here? All right for me to come to my own gig, is it?'

Noel, initially perplexed at his brother's angry tone of voice, shrugged his shoulders. Sure. No problem.

'All right for me to be at my own gig, is it?' Liam challenged again.

'Of course it is,' Noel testily replied.

'Sure about that, are you?' Liam retorted, 'because if I meet one cunt who says it's not all right I'm going to fucking do them.'

Noel now knew the score. Hold mouth, deep breath, walk. The way to keep the good ship Oasis afloat. Worked so far, as well. Noel shook his head as if to say, You dick, and he stepped away to the dressing room.

"That's it,' Liam shouted at his brother's back, 'fuck off somewhere else, you cunt.'

Then those eyes, covered by sunglasses that were wholly inadequate to stop the heat rushing out of them, turned on me.

'Do you know what?' he snarled, 'he only called me last night because my ma asked him to. That was the only fucking reason. He doesn't care about me. He doesn't care about anybody except himself.'

Normally, when he was laying into Noel, I simply made mental notes. That's my job. But this time something inside me just couldn't let it pass.

'Liam,' I said. 'Why the fuck did you do that? He's 20 minutes away from going onstage and singing alone in front of 8000 people and you're giving him shit like that.'

Liam looked me up and down. Then he let go. 'Oh, you can fuck off as well, you cunt. I'll fucking leather you anytime. I don't care who the fuck you are.'

'I know you don't, but that ain't the point.'

'Nah, you shut your mouth, mate. 'Cos if you don't I'll shut it for you. OK?'

'OK.'

'He's a cunt and so are you. And if I want to come to my own gig I fucking will. All right?'

'Never said you couldn't.'

'You better not. I'll do any cunt, me. I don't give a shit.'

He stared at me for ten seconds. Waited for a response. But I kept silent. Nervously silent. Truth is, I felt out of my depth. I felt as if I had just overstepped some invisible line. Other members of the band could challenge him but I was an outsider. This was his ground. This was Oasis territory.

Touring seduces you like that. You join an army and soon you start believing it's all for one and one for all. I'd seen examples of it already. People acting like they were in the group. Inwardly, it had made me smile. I wasn't laughing now, though, and I certainly wasn't about to start scrapping. Truth is, it ain't my game. Never has been, really.

I tried to concentrate on Travis and Liam walked off. About a minute later the inside of my stomach stopped rattling.

*

Mouse had been verbally threatened. I had been physically threatened. Someone was due a punch that night.

Mani is the bass player with Primal Scream. He was once in The Stone Roses, a band whose importance in the making of Oasis can never be overplayed. He was in Dublin that night, had come to check the show. Mani was standing outside the dressing room as Oasis launched into their encore. He wore a leather jacket, leather trousers. He had a keen face, striking eyes slightly covered by his blonde fringe. Leading up to the room that Mani stood outside was a small corridor. Liam and Terry now walked up it.

Mani was the first to see them, shouted a cheerful greeting to Liam. But Liam angrily shouted back, 'I hope you've got some bullets on you.' And before Mani could reply, Liam had literally launched himself upon him, trying to get a headbutt in. The two men grappled each other to the floor, where Liam started trying to land punches on Mani's prostrate body. Terry swiftly moved to part them. The boys scrambled to their feet but Terry kept them apart.

Mani was more in shock than anything else. 'What the fuck are you doing, man?' he cried. 'What's your problem?'

'You fucking know,' Liam said. 'You fucking know.'

'I don't fucking know,' Mani protested. His eyes were wild with disbelief.

'Yeah, you fucking do,' Liam replied.

Terry now ushered the singer into the dressing room, closed the door, leaving Mani outside, bewildered and bruised. Mani turned to the rest of us and shouted, 'What the fuck was that all about?'

None of us could answer.

A minute later Terry came out, told Mani that Liam wanted to talk, smooth things over.

'Fucking right,' Mani said.

He followed Terry into the dressing room. And the door softly closed.

*

'He's gutted about what he's done,' Danny said. 'He is absolutely gutted. I've never seen him like it.'

It was the next night and we were sitting in the bar of Glasgow's Holiday Inn.

'So where is he?' I asked.

'Well, he wants to chill out,' Danny explained, 'be on his own for a bit. Just calm down and get some peace and quiet.'

'Don't say anything,' Terry confided, 'but he's gone to a hotel over in Loch Lomond. He'll be all right there. He'll get real peace and quiet there. It will calm him down.'

'What, you mean the hotel that Paul Gascoigne lives in?'

Terry held his breath for a second and then he put his head in his hands. 'Oh, my God,' he said.

*

Earlier that day Noel, Guigsy and myself had risen early, travelled to Glasgow before everyone else. We wanted to see Liverpool beat Manchester United that morning on

Sky TV. Instead United cruised it, so we went out shopping for records. Phil Smith had put us onto a good place. Fopps Records. We located it, got to work. Guigsy bought heaps of Lee Perry, I stocked up on some funk, bought Noel some Stevie Wonder.

As I paid by credit card, Guigsy and Noel stood by the door waiting for me. Whenever anyone walked into the shop they'd stop them and say, 'You on the guest list, mate?' The customer would smile. Then drop their jaw in amazement.

We went into the centre of town, looked around. Noel went into loads of shops but seemed to buy little. As we walked towards the car I asked him why. Noel simply said, 'I've got it all.'

*

I had just come out of the backstage area when it happened. And for a minute or so I stood there, confused. There had been no announcement. Nothing. Oasis just stopped playing, downed their instruments and walked. This was some 50 minutes into the show, after a half-sized vodka bottle came flying out of the audience and hit Bonehead smack on the knee. The band looked at the bottle rolling around the stage, looked at each other, nodded and then quit the stage. If there was one rule the band strictly adhered to it was this: you throw anything at them and they go. Ta-ra.

The band walked offstage and into the cars that had hastily zoomed up to meet them backstage. When the crowd finally realized that the gig was actually over, finished, Oasis were back at the hotel.

Meanwhile we had all rushed backstage. The crowd were starting to turn ugly. The road crew, experienced in such matters, now told everyone to stay behind the stage or go to the dressing rooms.

'The coins will start coming over soon,' Spooner, Bone-head's guitar tech, told me. We heard some glass smash against something, and as he gave me that told-you-so-look, I headed for the dressing room.

*

I opened the door to a room partly illuminated by a silent television in the corner. I fumbled for the switch and flicked it on. Instantly, someone shouted, 'TURN THAT FUCKING LIGHT OFF.' I did as I was told. Swiftly. Then another voice said, 'I don't know why you're bothering. What about the fucking television? The cunts will see that.'

'I know,' whispered another voice, 'But we can't find the remote in the dark.'

"This is fucking stupid,' said another, and the lights went, back on. In the distance you could hear the angry crowd singing, 'We hate the English, we hate the English.'

It was not that scary, but it was enough to make you wonder.

We stayed until the venue was finally emptied and vans had been secured to get us out and back to the hotel. Once there, we headed for the hotel bar. Outside, the police were guarding all the entrances.

There was an excited mood in the air. The other residents couldn't work out if they were outraged or thrilled by this unexpected turn of events. And then Oasis walked into the large bar area and the entire place went silent. Everyone put their eyes on the five musicians, watched and waited to see what would happen next.

But nothing did. The band sauntered up to the bar and ordered drinks. People started talking, softly at first. And no disaster befell anyone. No irate fans stormed the hotel. No guests attacked the band or vice versa. No band or crew member got into a fight.

In fact, 20 minutes later everything was back to normal and we would now have the next day's papers to tell us all about it.

And Bonehead said to me, 'Imagine if that bottle had been just three feet higher. I wouldn't be standing here now.' He was right, home would probably be intensive care.

*

The next night Oasis walked through the phone box and onto the stage pretending to dodge imaginary bottles. It took a few seconds for the crowd to get it.

*

Behind Huw at the mixing desk stood the lighting guys, Mikey and Dave, with their headphones and their cigs and their computer-generated light show. Behind them was Julian, with his videos and projection, and every night Carole, the sound tech, would also come into the small compound.

They were supplied with a bucket of beer, soft drinks. And they were generous with it, always offering drinks to friends or family who watched the show from this vantage point. But when they saw Paul Gascoigne and his mate Five Bellies walk in, that generosity quickly evaporated. They all dived for the box and grabbed as many beers as they could before Gazza spotted them.

*

So many similarities. Working-class, talented, offbeat, North of England, drinking, football, money-makers, cultural icons living in a pressurized vacuum – no wonder Gazza and Oasis hit it off famously.

Noel had met him at Wembley. They had joked about each other's bank accounts. Now Gazza was in the dressing room and he was drinking everything in sight. He went from beer to sherry to shorts, didn't make a difference what was in the glass. He looked fit, though. Suspended for five games, he had shown up with Five Bellies, who said of Oasis after the show, 'Never seen anything like it. We normally go and watch the likes of Simply Red, Chris Rea, but these guys . . . they blow your bollocks off, don't they, like?'

That they do, my lad, that they do.

*

Gazza and Five Bellies called Liam up at ten the next day after being on the piss most of the night.

'What?' drawled Liam.

'Got a drink for you down here, like,' Five Bellies said. 'It's your favourite tipple. Triple Jack Daniel's and Coke.'

He could hear Gazza laughing in the background. Liam moaned, turned over and went back to sleep. Nutters.

*

Paul Weller was also staying in the hotel. He was playing Barrowlands that night. All his band and crew had come to see Oasis but he had opted to stay in.

The next day Liam met him in the hotel. They went and had drinks. Liam said to him, 'I'm the best songwriter in England!'

Weller replied, 'You don't write songs. How the fuck can you say that?'

'Because if I *did* write songs I would be the best songwriter in England.'

*

Tuesday morning, 9 December, we fly to Wales. In the departure lounge, all of us, waiting with hangovers, hear a familiar voice. It is loud, assertive.

'It's all right, I've weathered the storm. I was on the road but I handled it.'

Noel looked up from his *Viz* comic and wearily announced, 'I think it's psychedelic Liam this morning.'

But it wasn't. It was a coming-down-from-the-night-before-and-who-wants-a-tongue-lashing? Liam. He'd already got Bonehead, caught him buying Paul McCartney's biography at the airport. Ripped the book out of his hand and lobbed it over a balcony. It had landed on a table taken up by stewardesses. One of them called security. But Liam evaded him, made his way to the first-class lounge.

Bonehead now walked in.

'And what the fuck are you doing buying a Quacka book?' Liam roared. (Quacka was Liam's surreal nickname for McCartney. Macca becomes Quacka via Wacca.) 'Quacka the wanker. What the fuck do you want to read that for, eh? Fucking Macca the Quacka. Good songwriter but a right wanker and you bought a book on him. You bought a book on Quacka.'

The level of disgust in his voice could not have been more prominent.

'It's only a book,' Bonehead protested. 'It's not like I'm moving in with him or anything. Jesus.'

'But it's Quacka,' Liam shot back. 'You can't buy his book, you dick.'

Liam then noticed Noel looking out of the lounge window, turned his attention to him now. 'What do you think, Noely G? Eh? I love you, Noel, so tell me what you think. Come on.'

Noel ignored his brother.

'Scaredy cat. Scaredy cat.'

Noel glanced up at Liam, not happy.

'Come on, Noel,' Liam insisted. 'I love you, so what do you think? I know, I know, answer this instead. What are you thinking about right now?'

'I'm thinking about music.'

Liam couldn't find an answer to that, backed off from his brother, turned to Bonehead and said, 'Fucking Quacka!'

Bonehead's eyes raised. It would be a long flight to Wales for him.

*

A long day for Terry as well. Liam hits the hotel bar in Cardiff, raging. Starts going up to people saying, 'Are you Welsh? Well, I fucking hate the Welsh.' No one responds.

There are some journalists present, sneaking around. They're pointed out to the singer. So Liam throws a pint of beer over one of them. 'I fucking hate journalists as well,' he snarls.

*

The next day Iggy and his mate arrive at Cardiff's International Arena, hang out backstage. Again they bring stories of mutual friends, all of whom seem to be in some kind of shit again. This little piggy is going to court for exposing himself ('but everyone knows he's always getting his hampton out in the pub,' Iggy protests) and this little piggy has just had his eye gouged out. Iggy mentions a couple going through a real bad time. A now sober Liam remembers them.

'I was in this club having a drink with them,' he recalls, 'quiet pint, like, that's all it was, and suddenly, for no reason, he lamps her, double fucking hard. I'm like, Hang on a minute. Then she turns around and whacks him just as hard. So he whacks her back and then this geezer sees it all going off, so he steps in and whacks the guy. So the girl then whacks the guy and suddenly there's fights breaking out everywhere and I'm sitting there going, No, no, all we want is just a quiet pint.'

Manchester.

*

A strange occurrence indeed. Three numbers into the set and there is a commotion sidestage. Steve Strange, the ex-musician and club owner, has appeared out of nowhere and is loudly shouting to Liam.

Liam hears him, turns toward him with a face that says, Like, I'm playing a gig here, mate, can't it wait? Spooner and Roger step in, remonstrate with Strange. But his message seems so urgent, he refuses to budge. Keeps shouting. Security arrives. And that's the last we see of him.

*

After the first Cardiff show, Noel told Rob he was going to have just the one drink and then call it a day. But then he had a drink and another and at seven that morning Noel was still on manoeuvres, still on dawn patrol.

Meanwhile I was backstage talking to Johnny Hopkins, the Oasis press officer. Album Of The Year lists were starting to pop up in all the papers now. Oasis were struggling to keep Top Ten. It was between The Verve and Radiohead. After that it was anyone's game. They don't stand a chance in the press,' Hopkins said of his group. 'Do you know what one *NME* editor once told me? He said he hated Oasis because they reminded him of the bullies in his class.'

*

Mike Rowe drops his trousers. He has on lime-green underpants. Bonehead takes one look and says, 'Oh, I like them. Can I have them after you've finished?'

Mike takes off his glasses. As he starts wiping them, Noel says, 'I'm going to play you some Joy Division now and if you don't like this I'm going to larrup you big time.'

'Yeah, yeah,' Rowe mutters. 'And then you'll sack me.'

The tour goes on but the running gags are always the first to show wear and tear, to start wearing thin.

*

The next day Noel travelled up to Manchester early. He wanted to see Paul Weller play The Apollo. Noel didn't seem to mind that throughout their three-year friendship Weller had witnessed only two, maybe three, Oasis gigs, didn't seem to mind at all.

'Course I'm going to see him,' Noel explained, 'precisely because he won't come and see my band. And you know what I'm going to do? I'm going to sit sidestage with a pail of headphones on, reading the newspaper, shouting, "Rubbish!" after each song. That's what I'm going to do.'

*

Oasis playing Manchester threw up a million security problems, put a million people on their case. Threats and guest lists. Steve Allen, advance security man, had put the word out to the band: don't worry. It's all taken care of. Fences were being built, all-night security guards with growling dogs were being employed. No problem, no problem. Bullshit. Of course there were huge problems. This is Oasis. But Steve didn't want panic infecting the tour. So he kept on smiling.

Naturally, the hotel was stuck right in the wilderness. Again, old house, big grounds. This was their home town but this time around not one person complained about being hidden away. Strange to see Oasis glad to be invisible.

*

That Saturday morning I went walking alone in the grounds, to gather my thoughts. Liam saw me from a car window, waved. Later on he said to me, 'You're a weirdo.' For Liam, weird is wanting to be alone, because his fear is being left alone.

The cars they normally travelled in were sent on a dummy run and the band boarded a specially hired coach.

'It's a bit much,' Guigsy pointed out, 'a bit paranoid sending us in a coach and not the cars. Bit over the top.'

Liam agreed. 'Look, if we're going to get done we're going to get done. Doesn't matter if we're in a coach or not.' He shrugged his shoulders. Logical.

We drove past Peter Street.

'That was our first rehearsal place,' Bonehead informed Marcus. He kept looking out of the window. Five minutes later we drove up the City Inn Road. Bonehead, again, to Marcus: 'Do you remember when we first met you? It was that pub there, opposite the Hacienda. And what for? All so you could pay your mortgage.'

'In cash,' Guigsy put in.

*

Noel sat at the canteen table and said, 'Top one last night at Weller's show. Thought I'd got away with it but fucking Weller goes, "And now we have a very special guest." And you know what he goes into? "Woodcutter's Son", and of course once again I'm standing on a stage, pissed as an arse with Paul Weller in front of thousands of people, mouthing to him, "What key is this in?"'

*

In the dressing room with Travis, Liam announces, 'I should do a fucking book. I know what I'll call it. I'll call it *I Was The Quiet One*.'

Two Manchester gigs, one word: stupendous.

*

I get in Noel's car and we drive back to the hotel. The driver has the radio on. Top 40 gear. Gotta keep an eye on it all, says Noel. As we turn into the long drive, the songwriter peers into the darkness and asks, 'Where's the fucking security they said they were going to put on the gate? Oh, I know,' he said, mixing bitter with irony, 'We've only sold five million albums. I don't suppose we're worth it now.'

*

Three dates left now, at cavernous Wembley. The place is sold out and the band perform and the crowds clap and there's noise and life but there's something missing. Surprise, tension and danger. Something missing from the centre of things. Noel is feeling it as well.

These Wembley shows, it feels like a job now. And he won't complain because after all the crap jobs he's had, he knows a good thing when it comes his way, and he won't disrespect those he left behind in that work by griping about his new employment.

'Where's Meg?'

'Not coming. That's how bad it is these days,' he says smiling. 'Not even my own missus will come and see us.'

*

In the dressing room Noel asks, 'Anyone seen the new *Fast Show* series? Fucking top! Good as the last series.'

'Don't like it, me,' Liam says. 'It's a bit like *Be Here Now*,' he adds cryptically and with a small grin.

'How do you mean?' Noel enquires.

'You know, prefer the last one.'

Even Noel was left speechless by that quip. And broadly smiling at his cheeky brother.

*

And then it was Christmas. Then it would be January. And that meant America. And that meant thinking Oasis 24 hours a day once again. But now, as the last notes filled the Wembley air, it was lockdown time.

*

On New Year's Eve a young, good-looking chap approached Noel Gallagher and asked him, 'What is the best thing that happened to you this year?'

And, without missing a beat, the songwriter replied, 'Marrying Meg.'

Four

BACKWARDS POP STARS
America

Owing to personal reasons, Paolo was unable to join Oasis at the start of their US tour. He met up with them in Vancouver on Saturday 24 January 1998.

True or false?
'Never resent a rock musician getting rich – the lucky ones deserve it for the gamble alone, for taking on this life and playing their music with no guarantee of anything except the probability of failure and exhaustion.

Richard Dunkley, sleevenotes to Argent's
All Together Now

I AWAKE in a large Vancouver hotel, pull back the curtains. Sheets of rain fly against the window and the wind punches and screams at the walls. Depressing. I call reception and ask what time the band are due in. Anytime now, they say.

Coffee. The papers, more coffee.

Finally I catch the lift downstairs to the lobby. This is where I bump into Terry. He tells me that – surprise surprise – chaos has again broken out. Noel's left his passport in a coffee bar in Los Angeles. He's been detained at the airport by Customs. He's not the only one. Guigsy and Mike Rowe were accused of carrying drugs and strip-searched.

Guigsy: This guy was going, 'We know you have drugs, just hand them over.' I was like, Really? And what drugs would they be? And the guy said, 'Cocaine, there's cocaine on your T-shirt.' Well, that's funny because I actually gave up cocaine two years ago and the T-shirt I am wearing was brought yesterday and put on brand new this morning. The dicks.

Noel: I was sitting there thinking, Top, I'm going to be at City versus West Ham tomorrow, ringing up Danny [a West Ham fan], going, And Uwe Rosier has scored . . . Another own goal for City.

*

The gig was indifferent. The acoustic set was the highlight. It started with 'Don't Go Away', went on to 'Talk Tonight' and finished with a ballad version of John Lennon's song 'Help' in which Noel brilliantly located the Beatle's pain, made it clear for all to see. 'Help me if you can/I'm feeling down . . .'

Noel sang it like the words were written for him right here, right now. And he would do so for the rest of the tour.

*

Attendance was poor. In an arena holding 12,000 seats, half of them were taken up. It would the only venue not to shift tickets.

'Well, what do you expect?' Phil Smith said. 'They only played two numbers the last time they were here. Then someone lobbed a shoe and they got off. I mean, at least in Glasgow they got an hour.'

Cornershop were now the support group.

Noel was feeling shit, so he fucked off early, but Liam stayed in the dressing room and said to me, 'Have you heard Ian Brown's new solo album? It will do your head right in.'

The album was fresh, brand new in the shops, but Liam had already memorized every song, every lyric, every nuance. Musically sharp, Liam, because Brown still commanded his attention, his respect.

Even a recent *Loaded* interview, in which Brown had badly dissed Oasis, left Liam unruffled. 'Yeah, yeah, I heard about that,' he said. Dismissively. 'Now check this bit out,' he excitedly commanded. Liam literally talked me through the album, pointing out all its colouring. It fully intrigued him how Brown would develop something of real musical worth and then instantly destroy it with weird noises or totally inappropriate chord changes.

At the end of the album, Liam asked me, 'What do you think?'

I answered, 'I really don't know. One minute it's . . .'

'Exactly,' Liam interrupted. 'You can't work out if it's absolute shite or if it's genius. Whether he's actually brilliant and taking the piss or just brilliant for a minute or two. And that I suppose is . . . top. Or is it?'

*

Noel was in a down mood by the time we got to Seattle. It was a subdued dressing room. Noel's mood infected everywhere. Heavy silence. But after the gig he smoked and drank and smiled and the tempo picked up again. It had been a good show but Marcus couldn't put away the band's recent Chicago performance. 'The crowd there,' he enthused, 'they brought tears to my eyes.'

*

Sunday night in San Francisco. Sue, her husband Marcus and me go to see Tarantino's new film, *Jackie Brown*. Noel has already seen it back in London at a Samuel Jackson NFT interview. (Later, the two of them met in the flesh at a TV show. Noel has the proud pictures to prove it.)

I found the film laborious. At coffee afterwards I told Marcus this but said my perception could be affected by jet lag. Marcus agreed but added, 'I always feel guilty saying I have jet lag.'

'Why?' Sue asked.

'Because,' Marcus said, putting down his cup, 'where I'm from people *dream* about getting jet lag.'

*

After the soundcheck in San Francisco, Noel and Marcus stood by the mixing desk, Marcus using his mobile phone. He said, 'OK, thanks' and clicked it off. He turned to Noel. 'I've just had a piece from the *Sunday Mirror* read out to me. You remember all the shit we had coming into Vancouver? Well, apparently Liam was so drunk in Vancouver he couldn't fill his visa in properly, and that's why they detained him.'

'But they didn't detain our kid,' Noel protested, 'They detained me.'

'And apparently,' Marcus continued, 'a limousine finally arrived to whisk the singer away to the gig, arriving just in time to perform to a sell-out crowd.'

'Sell-out crowd? It was half full. Wankers.'

'I know. That's what we should sue them on. Sell-out crowd? Fuck off, mate. No one was there. Two million quid, please.'

'Last time we played here,' Noel said, opening various doors backstage, 'the promoter put in a games room. But fucked if I can find it.'

We walk up some stairs. Still no success. Noel's getting annoyed, then confused. Then he thinks for a minute and it hits him.

'I know what's fucking happened,' he exclaims. 'We haven't sold millions and millions of albums, so he hasn't bothered this time. The cunt.'

So Noel went out and played an absolute blinder. Think I'm finished. Eh?

*

Another hangover morning filled with coffee and Anadin and small talk. We fly to Los Angeles, book into the Shutters hotel, which is by the beach, look at our spacious rooms for about five minutes, then turn around, get into vans and drive to the Universal Amphitheater. I'm in with Noel, Guigsy, Mike Rowe and Strangeboy. I'm feeling good, haven't had a cig for days now.

'Why?' Noel wants to know as our van slows to a halt in the mid-afternoon traffic. Freeway snarl-up and a pale sun is upon us. 'Because on New Year's Day I was sat there watching Celtic versus Rangers and this pain hit my chest and I thought, Enough is enough.'

'Listen, mate,' he sneers, 'I wake up every day with chest pains and I give a shit. And another thing: don't think it will make you live longer. Oh no. You'll get three years at the most, by which time you'll be in a wheelchair being pushed around by your daughter Sarah Jane with her kids behind her and all of them hating you for making them do it in the first place.'

Guigsy nodded sagely. 'Chief always makes sense,' he said.

'Is there any music in this van?' Noel wanted to know. 'I've got some,' Strangeboy said, grappling inside his bag. He pulled out a selection of CDs. Noel chose Simon and Garfunkel's *Sounds Of Silence*. 'It's a time this one,' he enthused about the title track. 'Check out the snare drum. Fucking mega.' The album continues but quickly wears thin. Next up, Led Zep's 'Rock And Roll'. Loud, demanding, thrilling music. The song finishes. Noel, with absolute admiration in his voice, enthusiastically shouts out, 'Good work, fellas.'

The Zep album stays put until we arrive at the gig. It occurs to me that this is the band that now exerts the biggest influence on Noel's songwriting. Big riffs, dancing beats. Way to go.

*

Tjinder and Ben from Cornershop watch Oasis sound-check. If they had any previous doubts about Oasis, then their personal contact with the band has ensured their swift departure. Both outfits fit well together; mutual admiration.

They're on a weed mission when Guigsy strolls into view and we retire now to the dressing room area. Liam joins us but he's too active to be around smoke. He can't sit still, some kind of nervousness. 'Fuck it,' he tuts. 'I'm off to mither some cunt.'

Guigsy smiles broadly. 'Wouldn't want to be that person,' he says. Then he takes another toke and leans back in his chair. Content.

*

Meanwhile Noel sits in the dressing room stuffing himself with KFC and experiencing extreme mood shifts. One minute up, next minute across and a little to the left.

Mike and Bonehead are at the piano in the dressing room. Mike is teaching Bonehead Billy Taylor's 'I Wish I Knew How It Would Feel To Be Free' (the *Film 98* theme). Bonehead keeps getting one note wrong.

It's one note too many for Gallagher Senior. 'Stop play-ing that fucking stupid tune!' he suddenly roars at them. The voice has true venom and authority. 'I'm trying to eat my fucking dinner.' He throws a half-eaten bone on the table. It skims the paper he's reading, lands by the ashtray.

'Chords, melodies, notes, fucking solos, I've had enough of it,' he yells with real exasperation. He looks over at me. 'I wish I'd been a fucking writer instead.'

He angrily flicks over the page of the newspaper in front of him and studies it. The guilty pair look at him, look at each other. Then Mike gets up to walk away but Bonehead grabs him. 'Oh no,' he says. 'Oh no. You're staying right here. If I'm going down you're coming with me.'

Bonehead puts his finger on a piano key and gently presses it. 'Here, Noel,' he gently enquires now he thinks the coast is clear, 'who would you sack first? Me or Mike?'

Noel doesn't even look up from his paper. 'You. I sacked that other cunt weeks ago.'

*

Five minutes later, change of mood. Bonehead: 'Noel, what do you think of this T-shirt? Do you think it suits me?' Big grin from Noel.

'I tell you what you look like. You look like a Paddy that has been on the dole for years and has just got his first pay cheque and gone out shopping for clothes.'

'Oh, fuck,' Bonehead replies. 'As bad as that, eh?'

Noel now sits at the piano, picking out just one melody and repeating it endlessly. Marcus comes in, starts sorting through some paperwork. Bonehead glances over at Noel. 'I wish you'd do something with that tune. You've had it for years.'

'I'm going to record it when we get off tour,' Noel reveals. 'Give it to that *X Files* film.'

'Yeah,' Marcus says, looking up, 'but for fuck's sake don't tell them that you've written it already.'

'No, course I won't.'

Mike looks puzzled. 'Why ever not?' he asks.

'You're not going to go very far in the music business, are ya, ya divvy?' Noel says, chiding him.

'You don't tell them it's written,' Marcus explains, 'because that way you can keep upping the price. You know, he really wants to do it but he hasn't got time at the moment. Of course, if the fee gets more attractive . . .'

'Ahh!' Rowe replies.

'Ahh!' everyone else says.

*

When you come off the Universal Amphitheater's stage, you turn right and you walk down some stairs. Now you are in the open-air guests' bar. As Oasis finished off a so-so show for a subdued audience, I walked this route. The bar was full. I heard one guy tell his girl that Oasis were absolutely awesome. He hadn't moved from his spot all night. Some things never change.

*

The next day Noel and I go record hunting. After picking up a good pile of tunes – Mott and Led Zep for Noel – we go on to a guitar centre.

'I'll only be a minute,' he assures me and the driver. In fact he takes at least 15 minutes to get back to the car. 'Happens every time,' he grumpily says, sliding into the back seat. 'Always some cunt who wants to talk to you and you can't get away from. And they never let you go. You're standing going, Excuse me but there's about 20,000 people waiting for me, but that's all right you carry on mithering me . . . Come on. Let's get to the gig.'

*

I think the gig that night is better. The group disagree. But Naomi Campbell loved it. She sat with Liam, simply dressed in blazer and jeans, in the back dressing room discussing and dissing a mutual acquaintance. 'He came up to Patsy at a party once,' Liam reminisced, 'and said, "The reason I'm gay is because of women like you." I said to him, "Come here. Now look, you fucking divvy, I don't give two shits about you being gay or anything fucking else. But you ever talk to Pats like that again and I'll kill you."'

Naomi said, 'I'm taking some time off soon.'

'What you on about? You've just got off holiday,' Liam said, teasing her.

'I know, but I've been doing this since I was 17 and sometimes enough is enough. I want to get into something else. It's not like I need the money.'

'Don't fucking do anything for money,' Liam snapped back. 'Do that and you're finished. Money's crap. I can't wait to live in a place where it don't mean nish. Imagine living someplace where you pull out a grand and they say, Doesn't mean anything here, mate.'

'Sounds like heaven,' Naomi said with the cutest smile.

Johnny Depp wore his hair white but kept his hand outstretched and invited everyone back to his yard. He lived in Beverly Hills, in Bela Lugosi's old house, and he and Noel were old friends. Depp had played on two Oasis records (their version of 'Fade Away' for the *Help* project and slide guitar on 'Fade In/Out') and Noel had taken to calling him 'our generation's James Dean'. The title didn't suit Depp. He's far better and it's a different time. But Johnny got the drift. Noel dug him because Depp had stuck to his guns. He'd come off a cute TV show, *Jump Street*, and not cashed in on his looks. Instead he got serious about his craft and cut his own path. Noel always had time for those kind of folk.

Rick Rubin and George Drakoulias were also present at Depp's house. They shared similar physical attributes. Big men, long hair, unruly beards. There was talk of them producing Oasis's next album. Nothing concrete at all, but the two camps had started sniffing each other out. Rick was now in the studio with The Smashing Pumpkins, George getting ready to work with Kula Shaker. Naturally, George had no idea about the furore Crispian Mills had caused in the UK with his comments concerning Nazi symbols and related matters. And of course Noel eagerly gave him a blow-by-blow account.

This all took place in the main room, where Depp had built his own bar. It overlooked luxuriant gardens that sloped down towards town. The view was panoramic and the room we stood in spacious, enticing. The bar dominated most of the space and on the wall behind it Depp had placed a sign that read: 'No spirits to be served to Indians after sundown.' It was Depp's reminder to himself. Stay on the beer. At all times. Spirits made him angry, made him violent.

A guitar was found and Liam was first to go. ''E' are,' he said to Rubin, 'cop for this song.' Rick sat on a stool and gave Liam all his attention, but Liam just played the same chords again and again and again. After a bit Rick plaintively asked, 'Has the song got, like, a melody?'

Liam nodded. He said, 'It has but I'm not going to play it to you.'

'Oh, OK.' A pause. 'Eh, why not?'

'Because it will blow your fucking mind.'

Rubin looked perplexed. 'OK. Um. Do you have any words?'

'Same thing,' Liam said, strumming away. 'Can't do it. Because the words will also blow your mind.'

Rubin stroked his beard, like a wise man. 'It's great,' he finally said. I think he simply didn't know what else to say to get Liam to stop.

Liam put down the guitar, shouted over to his brother, who was talking to Depp, 'Noel! Noel! Play that tune. Play them that tune.'

'What tune? I've got millions of the fuckers.'

'The one from the dressing room, the one you played me there. Come on.'

Noel pretended not to know, screwed his face up as if counting down all the titles in his brain.

'You know it, the upbeat one.'

'Oh,' said Noel, 'that one.' Then he reached over, pulled the guitar to his chest and delivered a new three-minute song. It was in the vein of 'Rocking Chair', instantly recognizable but decidedly the sole property of Gallagher. Liam clapped along, shouted over to me, 'I want it to be our next single, get away from those heavy guitars.'

Johnny Depp led with the applause.

*

Later Noel told Rubin that there were only two American groups worth bothering with. The Stooges and the MC5. That was it. The rest was absolute shite. Noel said this with such certainty that you really didn't want to mention about 200 USA groups of a similar standing, not unless you wanted to start a sentence with the words, 'That is absolute bollocks . . .' and get into a five-hour drunken debate.

And I didn't. Not now, when the power of speech was fading.

*

Towards six, Liam and the others left for the hotel. The sun was breaking on our day off. Noel and I stayed on at the bar with Rob and Bruce, Johnny's assistant. Johnny himself was due on set – in *The Astronaut's Wife* – early that morning. He was saying his goodbyes. 'Yeah, fuck off and make some dough,' Noel teased him, 'while we drink your bar dry.' Noel had already written Johnny a note asking that Bruce stay with us, 'having it large'.

Bruce was a major Oasis fan. His favourite tune was 'Married With Children', from the first album. He wondered aloud to Noel what it was like to have so much money that you never have to work again. It was the sort of question we all want the answer to but never ask the very people who know. Why? Fear of embarrassment. Instead, we talk among ourselves and live for the lottery.

'Bruce,' Noel revealed, 'there is not one morning I don't wake up and think just how fucking lucky I am. Not one morning.'

'That's great,' Bruce said.

'And you know what else I love?' Noel asked. 'No one around me is a money head.'

*

Noel took a swig of beer. It was now nine and the day was already hotting up. He said, 'I'll tell you when I got to know the real me. It was when I moved down to London and I didn't know a fucking soul. I couldn't even work out the underground system. I was stuck in this small flat in Chiswick and it was the first time I had ever lived alone. I wrote loads of songs there. 'Some Might Say' came from that period. But every night and every morning I had to face myself and that was probably the most important time of my life, up until I met Meg.'

*

Noel and Bruce discover a shared passion for Pink Floyd's *The Wall* album. Drunk as skunks, they sing and air-guitar their way through the entire album. Then they put it back on and start all over again. I'm left thinking about the punk wars we fought against this band. And now? Well, either I'm too sensitive or else I'm getting soft, but yeah, there's some things on there. Noel was adamant that I should recognize the work. 'It's one of Lee Mavers' favourite albums, so that should be enough for you.' The Gallagher logic.

*

Depp's housekeeper, Mr Pink, arrives. Ironically, he used to work for the Floyd. He starts up a constant stream of Bloody Marys, keeps our fires burning. It's now daytime. Suddenly, out of nowhere, George Drakoulias is back in the room. For a moment I thought he'd been for a very long piss, but no, he left the pad about 12 hours ago, was popping back now because he wants to take Noel to meet The Smashing Pumpkins.

Now I'm in a car. Now I'm in a studio and it's somewhere in L.A. I can hardly move my mouth. Noel is still going strong. Unbelievable. It is six in the evening. Which means over the last 24 hours he has played a gig and drunk himself from here to eternity.

We meet Billy Corgan. He looms over us, we sway beneath him. He seems serious, not playful. He plays us a ballad song he's working on. Then we go next door and meet the other Pumpkins. Noel won't stop talking. He just dominates the room.

'How's Liam?' someone asks him.

'He's fucking top. But don't tell him that.'

'What you been listening to lately – Beatles still?'

'Not so much. And never the early Beatles. I mean the early Beatles were crap, bag of shite. It's only when the drugs get more interesting that the music does. But all that "Love Me Do" gear. You having that? I'm not having that. It's rubbish. Here, is there a bog anywhere?'

'Uh?'

'Sorry, rest room.'

'Oh, sure. Out there, turn right.'

Noel exits. In his absence, one of the Pumpkins' entourage says, with a voice dripping with irony, 'Well, I won't be listening to the early Beatles ever again.'

When Noel comes back in the room Billy Corgan tells him he wants to take him for a ride in his brand-new sports car. I spot my chance and get a cab phoned as the two musicians leave to go roar up and down some highway.

By the time they get back to the studio I'm in my hotel room watching the world spin around and around. And on and on. And so on.

The next day we gather in the lobby. I spot Noel. 'How you feeling, boss?'

'A tad tired,' he replies.

*

Meanwhile, after leaving Depp's house, Liam, Phil Smith and Alan White had slept, risen and then gone out to local bars. There they had got into scuffles, shouted at people, done some pushing and shoving. 'Right mayhem, top night,' Liam approvingly said. Vans were waiting outside. First to the TV studios of *The Ivory Keenan Waylon Show* for two performances, 'Don't Go Away' and 'Acquiesce', and then to the airport, to catch the plane to Dallas.

At the studio, Liam walked around his dressing room, shaking his head in disbelief. 'I want my bed,' he moaned. Then he paused. And really chided himself. 'I don't know what the fuck is up with me, wanting sleep.'

*

In the Bronco Bowl's dressing room in Dallas, Noel closed the *NME* he had been reading and shook his head. 'Have you read the *NME*'s review of Ian Brown's album?' he asked me. When outraged, it's noticeable that his voice goes up an octave. 'I don't know what's weirder,' he continued. ''The album itself or the geezer writing the review.'

'Liam can't make his mind up about the album, whether it's good or bad,' I told him.

'I don't have that problem,' Noel said. 'I know it's shit.' Then he put on a cowboy hat and started doing Deputy Dawg impersonations.

He didn't usually fuck up but 3200 Dallas people were treated to probably the worst guitar solo Noel has ever performed in 'Don't Look Back In Anger'. When the first bum note screeched out of the speakers all the band looked at him as you would do when you hear a fire alarm go off. Noel's response? To laugh his tits off. Onstage.

*

At the Houston gig, Liam announced Mike Rowe and Strangeboy as 'backwards pop stars'. The word 'backwards' was on his mind. Earlier, in the dressing room, Liam had heard one of the road crew assert a point and five minutes later go back on what he had just said. 'He's doing a Michael Jackson!' Liam exclaimed.

'How do you mean?' Mike Rowe asked.

'He's moonwalking. Going backwards on himself.' Then Liam started backpedalling, impersonating the wayward singer. 'Michael Jackson in the area!' he shouted. 'Michael Jackson in the area.'

*

You can't catch as many flights as we did without hitting one. Ours came as we flew into Miami. First there was a rapid, eerie darkening of the sky, then deep thunder followed by cracks of lightning, noisy rain whipping the window and then the plane tilting a little, trying to steady itself like a drunk leaving the pub and hitting fresh air. Way-hey!

The band were ahead in first class. They were whisked off to the hotel. By the time we got there the weather was such that you struggled to walk the few steps up to the hotel door.

The wind pressed on your chest mercilessly. Invigorating. But it looked like the Jamaica and Brazil game we had been given tickets for would be cancelled.

Wrong. As we drove to the ground we slowed down to avoid the mill of fans, both Brazilian and Jamaican. 'Do you think it goes off between them?' Liam mused. Noel had opted to stay in his room with Meg. They gave the band a box, the rest of us sat with the Jamaicans. But Liam and Guigsy were soon where they belonged. In the stalls. Shouting. Cheering. The game ended: one-all.

*

Back to the hotel. Liam went on the razz. Strangely enough, he spent some time in singer Bobby Brown's room. The next day he reported on the meeting. 'Fucking dickhead,' Liam sneered, 'He kept telling me he was going to change the music business. "Me and you, we'll do it together." Kept calling me his nigger. I was like, 'E' are, don't call me that. I don't like that. Not that word.'

When the two cultures clash.

*

The next day we drive to the gig about an hour away. Fran, Meg's friend, is on board now. She is talking about relationships. How boys can act out of order to a woman but their male friends never pull them up on it. Liam and I exchange glances. And don't say a word.

*

At the gig, in the canteen of the West Palm Beach Auditorium, Noel took one look at Spooner and said, 'Your face looks like someone has put a mask over a beach ball that is about to deflate.'

The next day we realized that we had but one weekend in America. That's how it happens. Home seems forever away and then suddenly it's staring you right in the face. A relaxed vibe started to settle in. Except for Liam.

Something was badly up with the lad.

In the van, driving to the Orlando show, Bonehead said, 'Liam was kicking off just now in his room. I heard him on the phone and then tables, chairs went flying everywhere.'

'Probably got the wrong number again,' Guigsy said.'

*

Roger Nowell, Guigsy's roadie, had been to see the doctor, got the news no one on this tour wanted to hear. Cut it out now or suffer soon and suffer badly. Noel was amazed. 'You don't go to the doctor's during a tour,' he exclaimed, ''cos what's he going to tell you? He's going to ask; Do you smoke? You'll say yes and he'll say, Well, stop it. Do you drink? Stop it. Do you take drugs? Stop it.

'What's the point? You go to the doctors on the last day of the tour and you say, Right, now is there anything you can do to fix my insides?'

This was the Mancunian way. You took on booze, chemicals and tobacco and you lasted the course. If not, get off the roller-coaster. Simple.

*

Noel Gallagher and Phil Smith. Both City fans. All their lives. Spent countless hours inside Maine Road. Moaning, mostly.

Noel: I spoke to someone the other day who said we played really well against Tranmere even though in typical fashion we drew 0-0.

Phil: Two games in a row and we're unbeaten. Could be the start of a run.

Noel: You know that's exactly what City should do. Draw every game of the season and get relegated. Not lose one game *and* still go down. That's the next thing for us.

Phil: Ain't it just.

*

At the soundcheck for the gig in Florida, the Central University, Noel picks up an acoustic guitar and plays his song 'Me And My Big Mouth', from *Be Here Now*. Now shorn of its workmanlike riff and slowed to ballad pace (a favoured Gallagher move), the song becomes a rueful and mournful rumination on the subject of fame. It really is mightily affecting.

Noel finishes the song, rests the guitar on his knees. 'Fuck,' he exclaims to no one in particular, 'why did I record that song electric?'

Then the answer hits him. 'I know. Because I'm a wanker who's taken far too many drugs.'

*

Noel Gallagher quote: 'When I grow up I want to be Neil Young.'

Some more Noel Gallagher talk. 'Noel, don't you ever cry with Meg?' 'Do I fuck. I did all my crying when I was 16 and 17.' 'Name me the five greatest-ever groups.' 'The Beatles, the Sex Pistols, The Who, Oasis, The Jam.'

*

After the last American show, which takes place in Atlanta's Fox Theater, not unlike the Hammersmith Odeon in size and layout, Liam is still not happy.

'Have you heard what's over all the papers in England?' he shouts. 'I'm having an affair with Helena Christiansen. I can't remember the last time I saw her and now,' he said, thinking of Patsy waiting silently and furiously for him at home, 'just when all I need is some peace and quiet, this comes along.'

'Sue the fuckers,' Noel said. 'You've got them.'

'No, I don't want their devil money. I don't want that.'

Impatiently, Noel asks, 'Well, what do you want?'

'I want them to print the truth. Not fucking lies.'

'You've got a long wait on your hands then, mate.'

*

Liam, later on: 'I should just get on a flight. Sack going home. Just get on a flight and go somewhere. Find an island, find some fucking peace and quiet.'

*

Noel was fine, relaxed. He stood chatting to long-term American fans who followed him where they could. I heard one ask, 'When you had nothing and Oasis weren't anything, did you ever get jealous of anyone in Manchester?'

'Never,' Noel firmly stated. Then he corrected himself: 'Actually, that's a lie. There was one person I was really jealous of because I couldn't understand how a fat Red wanker could get so far.'

No Christmas card for Mick Hucknall this year.

*

Liam sat alone in a chair. Pensive. Moody. Then something lively showed up but he still wasn't allowing fun to enter his mindset.

'You get what you want and everyone's going, Yeah, yeah and all that tackle, and then when you celebrate it, they call you a cunt. I tell you what, I've done my bit, had my say. Now it's someone else's turn, 'cos I'm sick of doing it for people. Sick of it. Let someone else have a go. Let someone else have the screams. I mean, if I was into all those girls screaming I'd be a pervert. All I want to know about is the music. See, I want it to be me screaming. I want to get excited by someone. I want to go to a gig and jump and down and go, Whee! Whee!

'Let someone else go on and have it. Pass the baton on. I don't want to be a rock star at 30. Who the fuck would want that? I've got to do different things, man. I've realized my dream. I've done it all. Had all the girls, had all the drugs, seen the world, played here, played in front of this many people, done it all. That's it now. Done and dusted. Now it's got to be for me. I've still got a bit more to say but it's someone else's turn soon. And me? If I make an album I'm going to make it for me. If other people dig it then great. And if they don't, I'm arsed. Because it's going to be all about me from now on. Me and no one else.'

It was the closest I'd ever heard Liam Gallagher get to making a retirement speech. And, as events turned out, one of his most prophetic. Because those words, 'me, me, me', would dog the last part of the tour.

*

It was Cornershop's final show. People were a touch sad they were on their way home for their own tour. But everyone knew that within a month they would know success. A good thing.

*

In the crowded dressing room, Noel found a chair and recalled his experiences in South America as an Inspiral Carpets roadie. 'Paolo, the planes there can hardly get off the ground. The only time in my entire life that I really thought I was going to die was flying one of those fuckers. We hit a storm and I thought this is it. There's no way a plane like this will land.

'It was so bad I was writing a goodbye note to my girlfriend. We got through that but that's just the start, mate. At the airports they'll steal your luggage. If you go down a wrong street they'll cut your kidneys out and sell them. The police will raid your rooms for no reason whatsoever and they'll put their guns against your head and there is absolutely fuck all you can do about it. It's also ten to one that the promoter will never pay you a dollar.'

'So why the fuck are we going?'

'So we can tell our grandchildren we did it.'

FIVE

HOLDING ON WITH BOTH HANDS

Australia and South America

Owing to an ongoing personal situation, Paolo missed the band's next five shows in Tokyo, Hong Kong and Perth. He joined them in Adelaide, Australia, as the furore over their behaviour on the plane from Hong Kong to Perth grew in the press.

True or false?
'What's the use of regrets?/They're just lessons we haven't learnt yet.'

Beth Orton, 'The Sweetest Decline'

THEY swear fuck all happened. Well, it did. But nothing to warrant the fuss being made. Christ, the way the papers were going at it, you would have thought they were a group of murdering psychopaths.

Yeah, they were drunk and yeah, they did get a little boisterous and yeah, they did try and smoke bifters behind the stewardess's back. But they didn't hit anyone. Or threaten them. And as for the pilot saying that he nearly had to divert the plane, well, that was just grand-standing. And if they had acted that bad, why did Cathay Pacific later issue a statement admitting the incident had been overplayed?

Anyway, just as the dust was settling, Liam – who else? – gave an interview to a journalist. Asked about the inci-dent, he vowed that if he found out the pilot was lying about diverting the plane, he'd stab him. Result? Cathay Pacific declared war, started discussing whether to permanently ban Oasis from all their planes.

Meanwhile Noel remained totally bemused by the fuss. 'I was genuinely asleep the whole time. I didn't see fuck all. Then I wake up and all of a sudden I'm public enemy number one.' Again.

Eyewitness report on Oasis walking through Adelaide airport: 'Liam Gallagher's only comment to *The Australian* could best be translated as "yeeaah-hhrrrgggh" while Noel, his songwriting sibling, strode straight through the mob waving his trademark Union Jack guitar over his head.

The Australian, Wednesday 25 February 1998

I have breakfast with Torsen. He works for Sony International marketing. I find him in the large dining room, where bright sunlight covers wide tables piled up with fruit and cereals, and this spacious layout, the warm colours, the healthy faces, it all makes you feel like you've woken up in a TV advert.

Torsen first worked with Oasis in Germany. Germany is important. It boasts the third-largest record-buying public. Torsen was charged with making the band successful there. He thought his task impossible. He couldn't see how he could sell a band whose fuck-off attitude took absolute precedence over their will to undertake the necessary promotion. 'But then the people heard the music,' he explained and shrugged his shoulders as if to say, 'What can you do?'

I told him that the reverse effect had happened with a couple of my friends. Ever since hearing 'Live Forever' I had been talking about no one else. But these guys remained impassive, unimpressed. It was only when Oasis appeared on the 'Brits' and insulted a million and one folk that my phone started ringing. 'That Oasis lot, you're right, they're OK, aren't they?'

Back in the days of 'Wonderwall' and Knebworth they were. But how about now? What were Sony saying about *Be Here Now*? They believe it to be a great success, Torsen replied. It will sell about eight million copies world-wide. That good enough for you?

It wasn't good enough for the people I'd been bumping into back in London. Julie told me before I arrived that her brother had been on the phone. He lived in Manchester and the word on Oasis was in the downwards direction. Too arrogant, too many bad words aimed against their home town. It's all right for them but we have to live here, he complained.

Pedro agreed, went further. Said the lyrics to the new songs were not focused enough. Too much stuff about fame or mundane lines about the weather. Paul thought that Noel was coasting now. Two good songs on the album. 'Magic Pie' and 'Don't Go Away'. That was it.

Another Paul said the album was too much like the old stuff. You'd waited all this time eagerly anticipating what they would come up with next and when it finally arrived it was the same old, same old. The songs were too long, too self-indulgent, too fuelled by the Devil's powder.

David agreed. Ask him about the '90s and he'll say there was only one group. Oasis. But *Be Here Now*? Sorry and all that. But not having it. The sound was too large. It deliberately covered up the ordinary nature of the songs. And so on. And so on. I remained unmoved and so did Torsen. Eight million Oasis fans can't be wrong, he said. 'But if they are,' I pointed out, 'that makes the next Oasis album a really intriguing proposition.'

'Paolo,' he replied in his thick accent. 'Every Oasis album is an intriguing proposition.'

*

Bonehead said, 'I'm mad to get off the beer.' And you could tell he really meant it. But it was impossible. He was surrounded by bottles and cigs and the people holding them came at you from all angles until you finally said, 'Ah, just the one.'

And then you were back on the roller-coaster.

*

I missed the gig in Adelaide, flew with the band instead to Melbourne. At the gig, Pete Barrett, a close friend who had moved out this way, said, 'In the past bands were one thing. They were rock. Or they were hippy. Or they were glam. Now they can be everything.'

He meant that Oasis could be as tender as they could be tough and it wasn't an issue, wasn't noticeable. Not in our time.

*

Back at the Melbourne hotel, a room has been set aside for the after-show party. Coyley had now joined the tour. He'll be with us until the end, by which time he will be married. Ruth and he will get hitched in Mexico. Noel, best man. Coyley is a United fan, fervent, committed to the last. He talks of them and of supporting your team as parents do of their families. You never leave your team. You devote yourself to them. For life, forever. Coyley is currently banned from Old Trafford. For swearing outrageously at the opposition before kick-off.

Noel is Manchester City. Big time. One time I saw him and Coyley argue the merits of their teams. If you didn't know about football, Noel's argument was so persuasive that he would have you believe that Manchester City were currently the greatest team ever and that Manchester United were a really poor second, destined for an isolated life in the lower divisions.

On the way home I said to Noel, 'Anyone listening would have thought that you supported the winning team.' He shook his fist victoriously in the air. 'That's the City way,' he declared.

It figured. Self-confidence, blagging, a refusal of present-day truth, they're requisite qualities when you're an unknown band living in poverty, rehearsing in damp basements but are intent on world domination and having every one of your rock-star fantasies brought vividly to life.

And now the City fans were strangely silent as their team slid further and further down the Nationwide table. There was no banter, no ribbing. Just a strange quietness. This, Coyley couldn't work it out. In all his years with Oasis, he'd never known anything like it. 'Barnsley beat United and they didn't say a thing, which means either they've got too much money or they're so depressed they can't talk about City.' He paused. Then his face lit up. 'Either way . . . it's fucking top.'

*

The incident on the plane happened on a Thursday. By Sunday, the day of the gig, a fried-chicken outlet were running TV adverts that featured Oasis lookalikes about to throw food around a plane. But our chicken is so good, said the advert, you'd never waste it.

*

At the party in Melbourne, Liam took control of the music. When he put on The Beatles' 'A Day In The Life', I looked around the room. Everybody – Australian, British, whatever – was either singing or unconsciously mouthing the words as they sat with friends, drinking, listening, gesticulating.

The Beatles, the real folk music of the world. Which is why you can't hold Oasis up against them. Of course, huge staggering success is the common denominator between the bands. Which is why – much to the purists' disgust – they get compared to the Fab Four. But will Oasis songs be so embedded in people's souls 30 years from now?

Impossible to answer. But that's the real test. And Noel knows it.

*

At the airport the next day, two young girls stood in a newspaper shop, staring at a picture of Liam in the paper. 'One day,' one of them avowed, 'I am going to meet him.' Liam sat but 20 yards away. Staring into a cup of nothing.

*

The band now travel separately to us. Most days; the first time we see them is on the plane when they're safely ensconced in their first-class seats. Coyley has named the rest of us 'the holiday-makers'.

When we arrive in Sydney the band are diverted to waiting cars, the rest of us take the normal route. I come off the plane with Huw, the soundman. In front is a TV crew. They want to ask passengers what it was like to fly for 45 minutes on a plane with Oasis. We pass them interviewing a middle-aged businessman. 'Disgusting,' Huw shouts as we walk on, smiling. The interviewer and cameramen note us, quickly finish their chat and now come running up from behind.

'Excuse me, excuse me,' the interviewer exclaims breathlessly. He is overweight, determined. 'Do you have any complaints about the flight you've just been on?'

'Yes,' Huw replies. The interviewer motions quickly to his cameraman, who hurriedly switches on his instrument. The interviewer places his microphone directly in front of Huw.

'Care to tell us what happened?'

'Disgusting is what I would call it,' Huw spits out, 'and I will never fly on this airline again.'

'You mean Oasis?' asks the excited interviewer. He's nailed them at last.

'No, that man you were talking to. Swearing, drinking, fighting like that. And he had on the worst suit I've ever seen.'

And we walked away, laughing.

*

Mid-afternoon, the hotel bar of the Sheraton On The Park. Me and Noel, Noel and I. The bar is huge. Outside, in the park opposite, day bums move large chess pieces around a large board. Those playing don't seem to have much money but the weather is hot, not uncomfortable. I keep thinking of grey London. And smiling.

Some of the band, notably Liam, have taken to wearing shorts. Never Noel, though. Always covered. He's starting to feel the pinch now. Some of the gigs aren't selling as well as he would like and the press are still hammering them for the plane incident, day in, day out. This strain he could do without it. It occasionally flicks across his face. He buys me a beer. Michael Jackson is playing through the speakers.

'Is this *Thriller*?' I ask, toying with the cold bottle. 'The thriller diller.'

'Which is better than being the failure in Australia,' he morosely jokes. It may just be the first time I've ever heard him say 'failure'. Wasn't in his dictionary a year ago.

'So are you really taking a year off?'

'Too fucking right. Maybe two. Give a shit. Sit and get fat and watch TV all day.'

'Right. And not write any songs?'

'No. Instead I'm going to make a very significant dent in my publishing money. I'm going to buy an island and blow it up. I am going to stand on top of a mountain with a spear in my hand and blow the fucker to pieces. That is precisely what I intend to do when I get home.'

'Another drink then?'

'Paolo, knock it on the head with the questions. I'm not in the mood. Here,' he says, slightly brightening up, 'have you noticed those burger places called Harry Jack's? They're actually KFCs but one of the burger chains bought the rights to the name in all these countries. Marcus told me. At first I thought, Bastards. Then I thought, That's fucking genius. So I said to Marcus, Run a check on Blur, Shed 7, Embrace in every country and then buy their names. That way we can nick all their merchandising money.'

'What did you think of the gig in Melbourne?'

Noel sighs, puts down his drink. 'You can tell we're getting to the end of the tour. I'm such a tosser sometimes. I'm onstage, I've got thousands of people there screaming at me and the band and all I can think about is a pair of shoes I should have bought earlier that day.'

*

Two days later Liam sits in the bar with Bonehead and Whitey. Day off. The night before they had played Sydney's Entertainment Centre. Not fantastic but a good show, good crowd. The Australian band You Am I were on support duties and Noel, especially, had become a big fan. I watched them but I couldn't see it myself. But Noel kept on and on. 'You'll get to like them,' he would tell me.

'No, don't do it for me,' I'd reply. 'Too much like early Jam.'

'What and Weller never ripped off anyone?' he spat back. Noel can tongue-lash good sometimes, catch you unawares with his sharp tongue, especially when he feels you contradicting him, deviating from his world view. Yet I felt his bitter words that night stemmed from another source and that was the unique tiredness that touring activates, the kind that seeps into your bones, is ever-present, is never fully shaken off.

*

Liam seemed OK, though. Today he was in an expansive mood, and as the lager slipped down his throat, it ignited the surreal side of his brain, guided his conversation. He was thinking now of Mexico. He imagined that as the band finished the last song of the tour there a UFO landed and whipped them off to outer space for further gigs, further victories.

'But I'm not going to visit Heaven,' he avowed. He took a gulp of lager. He was wearing shorts and a checked shirt.

His face was unshaven but his eyes were clear. 'A word of wisdom to you all,' he announced to everyone, Bonehead and Phil Smith being present. 'My friends, never go to Heaven. Never enter a place that has got gates. You know why? They'll only lock you up and throw away the key. I don't want to go to Heaven, I want to go to Free Land. I've been on the run from the angels all my life. I've been digging holes in clouds and running from those fuckers with wings. So don't think I'm off to Heaven, where they can slam the gates behind you and never let you leave. All right?'

All right.

*

Half an hour later. Liam to Bonehead: 'I love you. [then, pointing around the table] And I love you and you and you. And I'm not gay but I just wanted to tell you all.'

Satisfied, Liam drained his glass and we sat in silence, not knowing what to say. Liam looked at us and with a dark tone broke the silence and asked, 'So why is it that none of you cunts have ever come up to me and said, "I love you, Liam?" That caught us. Liam then paused for effect before saying, 'I'll tell you why. Because you're all cunts and I hate you.'

*

When I first got to know him, we argued about two things. London and the proper length that trouser legs should be worn at. He said Manchester, I said the Smoke. He said long, I said short. Now, pissed at the bar, I throw in a cheap shot about Liam moving down to the capital. Surprisingly, he agrees with me. London is top.

'When the sun shines,' he enthuses, 'it's mega and you walk down the road and there's all these geezers going [he adopts a cockney accent], "All right, Liam? How's it going, son?" You don't get that in Manchester. In fucking Manchester everyone is walking round really miserable with their heads down going, "Are you the singer from Oasis? Well, cop for this, you cunt."'

Now cut forward 20 minutes. Liam, again, on London. 'Fuck London,' he snarls. 'You get all these geezers in your face all the time. And if they're not doing that then they're trying to do you over when you're not watching. Nah, I'm not having it. Fuck London. Fuck watching *Coronation Street*, *Eastenders*, *Match of the Day*. Done it, seen it. Fuck normality. In fact when I get back to London I might just turn around and come back here. It's only 23 hours on a plane and I'm sure I could manage that. I've spent longer than that in pubs staring at the walls.'

*

We've now been drinking for three hours. Noel is still upstairs sleeping. Apparently he crawled into his room at about ten that morning. Liam meanwhile is busy making plans for his and the band's future. His idea is simple. Split up. Finish the band. That's right. Sacrilege and all that, but kill Oasis. It's got tired, boring. Fuck me, he says, even Noel has taken him over in the outrage stakes. Look at him slagging off Diana or that other shit he came out with about being as popular as God. That was mega stuff. 'I'm the dullard,' he states. 'Noel's become me. Noel's like, Kill this one, fuck that one and here you, cop for this.'

Nah, enough already. Kill the band but then, and this is the twist of magic, reform under a different name.

Like The Beatles tried to do with *Sergeant Pepper*. Same line-up, different name. Then come back fresh, exciting.

Write a load of new songs and then start off at the bottom. Climb that ladder. Feel that hunger again. But first things first. Got to get a name for the band.

Phil Smith: 'Sons of the Stage?'

Fucking top. That's it. Nick the title of that World of Twist record and book an appearance at the 100 Club or some other dive as The Sons of the Stage. Then show up and give it to them. How top would that be? And then, if you ever wanted to play the Oasis tunes, go back out as Oasis.

Liam is excited. Madly so. He tells Bonehead. Then he calls over Whitey, informs him of the plan. Everyone agrees. It's the way forward. Now there's only one obstacle. Signor Noel Gallagher. The Chief. Band leader. Songwriter.

Noel walks into the bar wearing denim and a hangover that stretches from his head to his toes. And then back again. He sits down and orders a large gin and tonic, says faint hellos to everyone.

Liam: Noel, got to talk to you about the band.

Noel: Not now, Liam, I'm feeling shit. Just let me drink this in peace.

Liam: Yeah, but Noel, it's important. I've got this plan, see . . .

Noel: No! Liam, let me drink this. We'll talk later.

Liam: But Noel . . .

Noel: Liam! Leave me alone.

Liam: Fucking typical. Every time I want to talk about the band you fucking blank me.

Noel: No I don't.

Liam: Then fucking talk about it. Now.

Noel: Look, Liam, just fuck off and leave me alone.

Liam: You telling me to fuck off?

That's it. Noel quickly stands and walks away from the bar. He looks as if he's heading for the front door. Secretly, he doubled back on himself and went back to his room. He was fuming. Smarting. That fucking brother of his.

Liam is outraged. He calls after him, 'That's it. Walk away. Don't talk about anything. Go on. Your fucking songs are shit anyway. I don't fucking need you.'

Then Liam slams his glass on the table and he too storms out. Terry is the first after him. I shout after his disappearing frame, 'Liam, come back!'

And then I hear Bonehead say to Phil Smith, 'Listen to Paolo calling after him. Doesn't he know that only band members can do that? The cunt.'

That warm feeling of collective drunkenness, the laughs, the closeness that alcohol weaves between people, vanishes in the instant. Like bad magic now. As if the day never happened.

*

I wake early the next morning. As I dress I realize that I can't remember a day when I didn't see Liam Gallagher with a drink in his hand. I also note that whenever Liam goes off on one it always involves religion. Heaven, the Devil, God. They bug the fuck out of the singer.

*

I enter the expansive breakfast room where business-men are already gathering to close deals, make moolah. Marcus Russell is sitting alone. Mid-40s now, Marcus, but looking good on it. Fresh-faced, hair receding maybe, but he's sprightly, often humorous in a deprecating manner.

In front of him is a *Record Collector* news story that has been faxed over to him. A tape containing some of Noel's earliest songs is to be auctioned at Christie's. The songs are pre-Oasis. An assistant who has heard the tape delivers a damaging comment. She says that a lot of the songs are better than anything on *Be Here Now*. They estimate a selling price of between four and six grand.

'Bet it will go for far more,' Marcus states. He is now preparing a press release. 'I'm going to say that until we hear the tape I can't verify anything. I'm also going to say that it might have been nice of whoever it is who's selling this tape to have the courtesy to send us a copy.'

'Says here,' I say, scanning the article, 'that the guy wrote to Noel offering to give him back the tape. But if he didn't receive a reply then he'd go ahead with the sale.'

'We never got a letter,' Marcus brusquely states.

The seller of the tape remains anonymous. He states that he befriended the 18-year-old Noel in 1985. The song-writer was then working on the building. At lunchtimes he would come round his house with his mates and hang out, feed themselves.

He added that they were close mates. So much so that Noel had given him the tape, got his opinion, shown him where his head was at. That's how close they were. He finally added that Noel had promised to buy him a house when he got rich. (Noted that: not if, but when.)

Marcus was worried about breaking the news of the tape to Noel. He knew it would upset him. A private man, as every true songwriter must be, he would not welcome his past being dragged up. And then sold to the world.

*

Noel had no choice. When Marcus later asked him if they were his songs, he said, 'Sounds like it. Anyway, give a shit.'

'We can always get someone down there to buy the tape,' Marcus said.

'You're joking, aren't you? Spend six grand of my money for my songs? My own fucking songs. That's wrong. I'm not having that.' And put like that – you had to agree.

*

We were waiting near the hotel bar to leave for Sydney airport when Noel announced that a brick had been thrown through the front window of his London house. That stuff in the papers he had said about Diana? The police put it down to that. A loyal royal, upset. Big time.

'You can just imagine it,' Noel said. 'Some cockney twat shouting out, "We love our Queen, so take that, you Manc wanker!" Top.'

*

At the airport I bump into Michael O'Connor, production manager. He tells me that the airline we are travelling to Brisbane with has strategically placed undercover security men on the hour-long flight. 'They got a bit upset the other day,' Michael explains.

'Why? From what I hear, that whole Cathay Pacific flight incident was blown out of all proportion.'

'So did this airline. But when Liam later said he'd stab the pilot that's when they got a bit upset. And worried.'

Ah.

We pull into the hotel in Brisbane. A number of press-men rush towards us to take pictures. The band struggle through them and Liam heads straight to the bar. He and Noel are still not talking.

I go upstairs and sleep for a bit. Then the phone rings. A guy I met in Melbourne wants to come over. I go downstairs and tell Guigsy, Mike Rowe and Coyley. The guy arrives. We go to my room with tapes and a beatbox, spark up. The guy starts asking questions and all the time I'm thinking, Is this guy a pressman, part of a set-up? I spend the whole night listening out for devious questions. Then he says, 'Well, thanks a lot, mate, see you at the gig.' And leaves. Paranoia sets in easy on tour.

*

I sleep late. As I drink coffee I wander out onto the balcony of my room. A beautiful sky, warm day. Look down. The press have not disappeared. Quite the opposite. Their numbers have greatly increased. Now there's a size-able crowd of them gathered outside the hotel door. Every minute or so one of them will look up and eagerly scan the windows of the room. I'm spotted but I duck backwards. Instinctively. Then I think, Why?

I dress, wander downstairs and then out onto Bris-bane's streets. The press watch me intently as I walk off towards a record shop. They can tell by my dress that I'm something to do with the band.

At the shop I buy Noel a copy of The Style Council's *Our Favourite Shop* album. Weller has asked Noel to play bass with him at a charity gig he's performing for the homeless two days after our arrival back in Britain. Among the set list is the Style Council song 'A Man Of Great Promise'.

Noel knows The Jam and Weller's solo career back to front. But the Style Council? Absolutely lost on him. All that makeup and swanning around on boats or in fields,

making songs without guitars. Not having that. No anger,
no comment.

I get back to my room and the phone rings. I think
it's the guy from last night. But it's not. It's Terry and it's
serious.

Fucking serious. 'You probably don't know this,' he
says in a voice racked with concern and not a little guilt,
'but it all went off last night.'

'How do you mean?'

'The tour, it may be off.'

'What?'

'We may be going home. Liam whacked a kid.'

'Joking.'

'I wish I was. He's got to go to court this afternoon. He
could be deported. Now it probably won't come to that but
there's press everywhere. Say nothing if anyone tries to
talk to you.'

'What the fuck happened?'

'We went out for a drink and this geezer just wouldn't
stop taking photographs. He was told eight times to stop
and he didn't. So . . .'

'This is a bad place to pull that shit. The law is heavy
here.'

'Don't I just know it.'

'What's the likely outcome?'

'It can go three ways. Either deportation, a big fine on
the spot or he's put on bail and he has to return later this
year or whenever. Hard to say. The police were all over the
hotel last night.'

Jesus, I thought. Last night I was looking straight at
that guy and the cops were behind me all the time.

'Oasis lead singer Liam Gallagher was allowed to
walk free from a Brisbane court on an assault charge
yesterday amid fears that he may never return to

Australia. The British rock star, who allegedly butted a fan near his hotel on Thursday night, was released on a $10,000 surety. He pleaded not guilty.'

The Courier Mail, Saturday 7 March 1998

Marcus Russell and Rob took Liam to court. They had to fight their way through the press outside. Initially they had asked to enter through the back door. No way, Liam's Australian lawyer said. For this, you go through the press. Not around them.

When the proceedings finished, Liam was taken back the way he came in. On the way out, one guy actually hit Rob. On his shoulder and with his heavy TV camera. 'Watch it, mate,' Rob told him.

Give a shit. You're in the way of a good shot.

Liam's lawyer was delighted. He said, 'See, I told you we should go through the front. Now we've got film evidence of the shit Liam has to go through.'

*

Marcus Russell was not as happy. 'There was real hate in that court,' he told me at the gig, later on that day. 'Real hate. See, they didn't know who I was and so I just wandered around the court and some of the things the coppers were saying, that told you who the forces against you were. And the press! When the prosecutor asked for bail of £100,000, they were all going, "Yes!" Our lawyer told us that a guy up on a murder charge the week before got half that as his bail. Can you believe that? A guy commits murder and it's not as bad as this Liam thing. It's mad.

'So I'm sitting there and they announce the bail they want and I suddenly thought, Oh, shit, I've only got 25 grand on me. OK. Keep calm. Make sure they don't see anything on your face. Keep looking straight ahead. But our lawyer, Christ, you want to see him in action. He's one of those young, going-to-the-top-and-don't-dare-get-in-my-way guys. When I rang him on Friday night. I said, "I've got a client and he's very high-profile."

'Ten minutes later he's banging on my door going, "Right, mate, get me a desk and a telephone and we're in business." So he gets the bail down to ten grand and the press are going, "Oh, only ten grand."

'I went to pay the bail and the guy goes to me, "Can you vouch for Liam?" Look, I said, I've seen Liam Gallagher give about 30,000 autographs and pose for that many pictures. I have never seen him be rude or discourteous to any fan. I'd put my life on that guy and I'm as keen to find out what went down as anybody else. And that was that.

'But Jesus,' Marcus said, and you really could hear the stiff weariness in his voice, 'we've only played a few gigs and this country has been relentless, absolutely relentless.'

*

And at the Brisbane gig, Liam looked totally distracted and sang so off-key that even I noticed. Noel cut the set short. And the band travelled back to the hotel in bitter silence.

*

The next day the press numbers outside the hotel had dwindled, but not by much. Liam's court appearance was still the lead item on TV and the story was front-covered on all the papers. Everywhere you moved the story seemed to jump out at you.

I wandered down to the record shop again. It had good stuff and was cheap. Noel, Bonehead and Coyley were sat outside a bar. Guigsy was there too. He was determined that we should all play football in the park. I didn't realize what he was up to. Until later.

*

We duly gathered in the park, offered the locals a game. Everyone played except for Whitey and Bonehead. 'You ever seen Bonehead play?' Noel offered by way of explanation. 'He looks like Bambi with a replacement hip.'

The press couldn't believe their luck. All weekend they had been denied the merest glimpses of the band. Especially Liam. He was the hottest story in the country and they couldn't get close. All of a sudden here he was just yards away, running around in shorts, laughing, shouting. The pitch was surrounded by press. One TV station even filmed the whole kickabout. Every kick.

After all the football banter in dressing rooms and buses all across the world, I was intrigued to see who could actually play the game. I knew Guigsy would be good. But Noel? On 20 fags and a good drink a day, running around and energetically dictating the show? Well, it happened. He sat at the back, an imperious presence. He expertly tackled all who came through to him. Then he would move forward with the ball, shouting instructions. The Chief.

Guigsy sat in midfield. He seemed a bit out of sorts until I noticed a familiar smell and a long cigarette cupped in his hand. After about ten minutes of pulling on it and then discarding it, he started picking up the ball and slowing the game down. He neatly executed twists and turns that bought himself space and then he sprayed the ball around, usually up to Liam, who of course was a selfish little bastard who never passed the ball and went for glory every time. Liam scored four times.

We won about 10-2 or something stupid, and we were exhilarated. Now I knew why Guigsy had been so adamant about playing. Football had brought everything back into line. The team vibe, that feeling of everyone pulling together, permeated everywhere. The tour had regained itself.

After the final whistle, Noel suggested we have our picture taken. He asked a photographer to capture the moment. We, sweating and dirty, posed for the picture, singing. As the photographer prepared to take the picture a rival snapper spotted him and rushed over, pushing him out of the way. 'I'm taking this shot, mate.'

'Bollocks you are.'

'You try and stop me.'

'All right.'

Then the two of them started trading punches. Terry immediately jumped forward, separated them.

'You fucking wanker,' Liam shouted at his bodyguard. 'What the fuck did you break them up for? They were just about to get a taste of their own medicine.' Liam was so bitter, so angry at Terry's intervention. It wasn't often that he got a chance for revenge. Now it had been ruined.

That night we sat by the pool and drank and listened to a tape of the forthcoming Oasis b-side album. At one point Terry and Rob jumped fully clothed in the pool and danced to the band's version of 'I Am The Walrus'.

After it had finished, Noel said, 'Put on that Led Zep tape. Sorry, but you're going to have to put up with me playing air guitar all night. I've become a right Zep head, me.'

'Stairway To Heaven' now played. Ironic. This was the first song Noel ever learnt on guitar. At the time he was barely a teenager, poor and living in Manchester. Now he was a multi-millionaire who that night would sleep under the large Australian moon, his face and name known all over the world, his life a testament to all kinds of possibilities.

*

Meanwhile Bonehead was smashing his room to bits. The anniversary of his mother's death loomed in front of him. Consequently he'd gone downstairs to the bar in a belligerent mood, bumped into a reporter. Something was said and that was it. Bonehead kicked off. Then he returned to his room to bum off the rest of his anger and hopelessness. Finally Whitey and Danny managed to coax him out of the room and then the hotel. They went off for a drink.

And came back quieter people.

*

At the show in Perth, Liam came up to Marcus and me. He was anxious for some truth about his future. He wanted to prepare for it. 'Come on Marcus, don't fuck around. What do you think is going to happen when I go back to court?'

Marcus sighed. 'OK. First off there will be a big fine. They hate you and they know you're rich. But that may not be enough for them and that's what you've got to be prepared for.'

'So what? Is it prison then?' Liam curtly said.

'I wouldn't go that far but I think you have got to think about some kind of community service.'

As soon as he said it, I laughed out loud. Couldn't help myself.

Liam demanded to know why. Naturally. 'What the fuck is so funny?'

'Sorry, boss, but I just can't see you helping some poor granny cross the road and then going off to cut someone's hedge on a Sunday morning.'

'Fuck off, you,' Liam said good-naturedly.

'Doesn't work like that,' Marcus gently explained. 'In community service you work within your job. Like Eric Cantona had to teach kids how to play football? Liam will have to teach kids about singing.'

'Will I have to wear a uniform?' Liam asked. Sometimes his naivety was so charming.

'No,' Marcus replied, and then he and I started laughing. He too was visualizing Liam in a stripy prisoner's uniform, ball and chain dragging on the ground behind him.

Liam instantly cheered up. 'Can I wear my Hush Puppy shoes?' he eagerly asked.

'Course you can,' Marcus told him. 'Wear what you like.'

Liam turned to me and he clicked his fingers in delight. 'I can wear my Hush Puppies. No fucking problem then.'

*

But there was. What Liam didn't know and what was worrying Marcus like a virus right now was the opinion of Liam's lawyer. He had taken Marcus aside, told him, 'On this court circuit there are 18 judges. Twelve of them would quite happily go outside with planks of wood and a rope and hang him. Let's hope that when you come back to this country for the trial we haven't got one of them. Otherwise you may not be home when you expect to be.'

*

On the way back from the gig in Perth, another so-so affair, Noel noticed a church that had been boarded up. It was called The Higher Thought Temple. 'Shame no one thought to pay the rent,' he observed drily.

*

On our last day in Australia, all the papers agreed. Get rid of these unwashed, ignorant hooligans. 'Farewell To Oasis Oafs,' the *Sunday Mail* said. 'Goodbye Oasis and good riddance.'

What no one had yet sussed is that 30 years ago they had said the same thing to two other British groups touring their country and they too had managed to upset a few equilibriums. Step forward The Who and The Small

Faces. Say what you like, but if nothing else, Oasis keep good company.

*

We travel to Auckland, New Zealand. Another gig is put under the belt. But it's quiet time. Back at the hotel Joe Cocker is sitting in one part of the bar, but no one is arsed except me. And I can't think what to say to him. Early night all round.

The next day at breakfast I sit with Strangeboy and Mike Rowe. They have hot news. It's always welcome on tour. Anything to upset the routine.

'Gossip has it,' Rowe conspiratorially says, 'that Huw is fucking off today. He's not doing the sound any more. He's had enough.'

'Is it to do with his dad?' asked Strangeboy.

'I don't know.'

'So who's going to take over?'

Before he can answer, Coyley appears. Sits, orders coffee. He missed last night's Auckland show due to illness. 'Still feel really weird,' he says, shaking his head.

Now Noel walks over.

'Good morning.'

'No, it's not a very good morning,' Noel replies. 'Coyley, can I have a word?' He and Coyley sit in the empty hotel bar and confer. It's obvious what's happening.

For the first time since Slane Castle, Coyley will help direct the band's live sound. He will replace Huw, who has indeed chucked in the towel. Another sound guy, Bruce, will also be drafted in to work with Coyley. The pair of them start in South America. Today we fly to Wellington for the last show of this troubled Australian/ New Zealand tour.

*

At Huw's last gig, the band run through their sound-check. Then Noel checks his acoustic guitar. He opens up with a slowed-down version of The Jam's 'That's Entertainment' but forgets the words halfway through. Then he goes into a new song, a ballad with lyrics concerning a bow and arrow. Now he moves into 'Fade In/Out', which he has totally revamped. It features droning keyboards with Whitey supplying conga percussion. Satisfied, Noel lays down his guitar, goes to his dressing room. 'See the paper today?' he asks when I walk in. 'Apparently it's down to Ocean Colour Scene or Blur to write the English soccer tune for the World Cup.'

'Didn't they ask you?'

'Probably, but I'd have turned them down. I can't think of any words for a song like that, except, "Go on, chaps, I'm sure you'll get to the semis . . . And get beat by Germany again.'

*

All day, since we arrived in Wellington, Liam had been in the hotel bar. Liam drinks fast and hard. Bang, bang, bang. One after the other. Lager. JD and coke. Lager. At one point he talked to a fan until he suddenly sussed the guy was a journalist, hunting for an interview. Before he could pull back his fist, Terry stepped in, had him ejected.

Liam arrives at the gig and he is smashed. Pissed. Gone. The world is lopsided. There is fire in his belly, anger in his eyes. He walks onstage with the band and no one notices the Christmas-cracker whistle in his hand.

Noel kicks off the opening riff to 'Be Here Now'. Liam goes to the mike and sings the first line: 'Wash your face in the morning sun.' Then he blows the whistle: twice. Beep! Beep!

Noel furiously swings his head towards his brother.

Liam sings the second line: 'Flash your pan at the song I'm singing.' Then he whistles again. Beep! Beep! Then he looks at Noel as if to say, 'Yeah and what the fuck are you going to do about it?'

Liam is wearing baggy shorts and a shirt that is open to the top of his stomach. He looks unkempt and he is swaying by the mike. The song ends and he ditches the whistle on the floor. Then he starts ranting at Gareth, who stands sidestage controlling the band's onstage sound. Liam is saying he can't hear fuck all, he's shouting and raging. The sound is the worst he's ever heard.

'Oi, Gareth,' he shouts, and he pulls out his wallet from his trouser pockets and publicly offers to buy new speakers. The band ignore him, go into 'D'You Know What I Mean?' Liam misses whole verses. Noel is not even looking at him now, but at the start of 'Cigarettes And Alcohol' his temper finally cracks. He starts playing that opening riff and then – bang! – Noel has thrown his guitar to the floor and stalked off. The band follow suit and the guitar lies crying on the floor, bleeding feedback.

In the catering area by the stage, Noel waits. First glimpse of Liam and he goes for him, swiftly places his forehead against his and screams, 'What the fucking hell are you playing at? What is your fucking problem? I want to fucking know.'

The crowd are booing now. It's touch and go as to whether they will see Oasis play that night. Noel keeps his head firmly stuck to his brother's forehead until he turns and walks back onstage to cheers, the chant of 'Noel, Noel'.

When Liam appears, the crowd restart their booing. The singer is arsed. He announces 'Cigarettes And Alcohol' and the band play a not-too-bad-in-the-circumstances version. At its conclusion, Liam viciously punches the mike and walks offstage.

Noel now sits alone and plays 'Don't Go Away' and 'Fade In/Out'. As he does so, Strangeboy comes and stands next to me by the side of the stage. 'God, I feel so guilty,' he blurts out. 'Liam was in my room most of the night and he was going on and on about how Noel will never accept a song from him.'

'He's done the same to me,' I explain. 'He's played me stuff on the guitar which is really beautiful but he just hasn't got the discipline to see it through.'

'That's exactly what I told him,' Strangeboy confirmed. 'I told him to put together a load of songs and *then* go to Noel with them. It's no good going with just little bits. That's no good to Noel. At the end of the night he was saying, "You're right, you're right." Now he's like this.'

'Don't blame yourself,' I tell him. 'This one has been building since that row in Sydney.'

'I tell you what,' Strangeboy stated, preparing to walk back onstage, 'it's hard to play music when your muscles are shaking and you don't know what is going to happen next.'

What did happen next was somehow the band got through the gig. Liam sang perfunctorily, threw in a few sarky comments such as, 'This is called "It's Getting Better, Man", and it's fucking not.' And Noel again cut the set short and disappeared from that venue faster than you could say, my fucking brother. The crowd filed out in silence.

*

One hundred pounds says that this gig on Tuesday 10 March at the Queen's Wharf Events Centre in Wellington, New Zealand, was the first concert ever that Noel Gallagher stood onstage with a guitar for over an hour and didn't say one word to the audience.

*

I walk in the dressing room. I'm expecting a wired-up, angry Liam. I'm expecting trouble, probably a haranguing of some innocent, his anger needing to spill out somehow. But I am not expecting to hear Liam say that Oasis are finished.

'Good gig, eh, Paolo?' Liam quietly says. He is slumped on a sofa, sipping on a beer. Sitting around him are Terry, Phil, Marcus and a shattered-looking Maggie. But the singer is cool and aware.

The dressing room is small and to one side is a room in which Marion, the wardrobe girl, has been working. A light stand lies smashed on the floor.

Liam addresses Terry. His voice sounds deep, slightly cracked: 'Can you make sure Marion gets all my clothes, 'cos I'm off to Mexico tomorrow.'

'I'll tell her,' Terry replies. Now Liam turns to Phil. 'Ah well, there goes Oasis, but didn't we have a buzz, eh? What a fucking trip! But all things have to end.'

Liam seems calm, resigned. Everyone else just looks shell-shocked. He now turns to Marcus. 'I want to have a band meeting,' he softly states. Takes a swig of beer. 'Ask them what they want.'

'What they want,' says Marcus equitably 'is to have you in the band.'

'Really?' Liam asks the question with feigned surprise.

"Then why is there no love there?' he asks. 'Why do I have to put up with the dirty looks? Why is that then? I'll tell you why. Because everyone's like, I've got two kids now, got a family to support. Well, I knew you before you had two kids and you should fucking remember that.' There is surprisingly little anger in his voice.

'It's just how people get through a tour,' Marcus explains. 'It's not . . .'

Liam cuts his manager off by raising his bottle in his right hand. 'The magic has gone, simple as that.' There is a tinge of sadness in his voice but he's working hard to cover it.

'Liam,' Marcus says. 'You know what everyone is going to say. They want you in the band. Oasis is not Oasis without you.' Marcus, too, sounds reasonable. He knows what a volatile nature he is dealing with. Liam may be acting coolly as he casually snaps the band of the decade in two, but, as we have seen, he can swing either way. In a minisecond. 'Well call a band meeting for tonight,' he says. 'All I want is a ten-minute meet and then I'm in the bar.'

'It shouldn't just be you and Noel.'

'No, no, fuck that. I want a band meeting. I want some answers. 'Cos I was looking for love tonight and I didn't see any. All I saw was dirty looks all night. I didn't see any love. I want to know why. I want to know what they want. Do they want a rock'n'roll star? Do they want chaos? Or don't they? It's up to them. Me, I'm off to Mexico tomorrow. But before I go I want to see if they've got the decency to talk to me.'

Unexpectedly, Liam now turns to me and holds up his left hand. 'Paolo, do you like my future ring?'

'What's a future ring?'

'Apparently, if it doesn't crack within a week you haven't got a future. If it does crack, you do.'

'And yours?'

'Mine broke within two days.'

It simply wasn't the place or time to tell Liam that in all probability it was not destiny or luck that broke his ring. It was the simple fact that night after night he had been viciously smashing his fist into microphones.

*

Phil Smith, as we pile into the van for the silent journey home: 'That's more like it, just like the old days.'

*

I go upstairs to my room and try to ring Noel. Constant engaged tone. I go downstairs to the bar to see what's happening. Nothing. No band, no tour personnel. I go back to my room and fall asleep not knowing which country I will be flying into tomorrow. Argentina or the UK.

Or whether there will be a band called Oasis in existence.

*

Early the next day I read a stinging review of the show in the local paper. Most of the blame is laid at Huw's feet. The crowd suffered a diabolical sound. Liam's wayward drunken behaviour is not neglected but he evades a lot of the shots.

Then, as no one else is up, I take a wander around Wellington's orderly streets. This is a quiet town, a placid place. Major eruptions on this scale seem out of place. If Oasis are to break then it should be in a major city. Not in a quiet waterfront settlement. I bump into Gareth and the stage manager, a small Scot by the name of Pete Bell.

'How's the band?' Gareth asks. Wind-up time.

'Well, Liam is still mad for beating you up after the sound you gave him last night.'

'Is he fuck,' responds Gareth. 'This is how it works. He calls me a cunt all night. I sulk all day and then at the next gig we both go, Arsed! I said to him last night, "Would you have preferred the system we had in Melbourne?" He said, "Yes." I said, "Well, that's exactly what you had last night."'

'You've worked with them long enough. What do you reckon will happen today? Home or South America.'

'South America. Without a shadow of a doubt.'

*

So, Marcus, home or away? In the hotel bar Marcus is looking relaxed, relieved. 'We're going to South America,' he states. 'We've got a job to do and we're going to do it.'

'So what happened? What stopped Liam flying off to Mexico?'

'Well, the band met this morning and it was all very positive. Of course; Liam kicked it off by blaming everyone, but within a minute he had to shut up and listen to the others. He couldn't do anything else.

'So he said he would stop drinking. I told him, Liam, you won't stop drinking but what you have got to do is stop drinking before a gig. It's what you did in the old days. Back then you never drank before a gig and that's what you have got to get back to. He agreed on that and now we push on.'

What Marcus didn't and, of course, wouldn't mention – and he'd be a terrible manager if he did – was that Oasis stood to make over a million pounds just from the South American leg of the tour. I think that statistic would have sobered up anyone.

*

Maggie sits with us and she looks absolutely exhausted. Her pretty face is crumpled with worry and regret. She has been on the phone all night talking with the promoters and officials in South America. She has already put in a million hours sorting out visas for the travelling party, which has now been slimmed down for practical reasons, and now she has another monkey on her back. Aerolinus Argentinus have informed her that they are currently in discussion as to whether they will allow Oasis to board their plane to South America. 'All we can do,' she wearily says, 'is go to the airport, fly to Auckland and find out if this tour is still on.'

And that's precisely what we do.

The deal, the airline said, was this. You can fly with us but we want you to know this: on the flight, accompanying you, are two armed security guards. Make no mistake: any trouble and they'll step in. 'Guys with guns on a plane,' Mike Rowe mused. 'Nothing like a hole in the roof to keep the oxygen levels up.'

'Yeah,' Phil replied, 'the only thing is, when those boys shoot, they don't miss.'

*

At Auckland airport I have dinner with Mikey, Roger, Clint and Pat, mainstays of the road crew. Mikey, the lighting guy, has already worked in South America, Rio de Janeiro to be precise. He was with The Happy Mondays. 'Absolutely mental,' he recalled. 'There was this rumour that the band were bringing 5000 Ecstasy tablets into Brazil. So at the gig Shaun Ryder and Bez got hold of all these laxative pills and chucked them into the audience.'

'Shit gig then,' Roger says.

*

On the plane to Buenos Aires, Oasis sit in first class and we sit in economy with cheerful Argentinians at the back. Good vibe. Liam wanders down, checks the party spirit and stays for about two hours, drinking, listening and singing along to some Irish tapes that Pat the rigging guy has brought with him.

Noel now appears. We strike a deal. I'll go to his first-class seat and listen to the *You Am I* album, he'll stay here and hang out. Done. An hour and a half later, I return to my seat. Noel's smoking, drinking, looking happy. 'What do you think of the album?' he enquires.

'Top. Nothing like their live set. It really is excellent. One song I didn't like and that was it.'

'Only told you about a million times you'd like them.'

Yeah, all right, genius.

*

Six hours later we land in Buenos Aires. And it's traffic-heavy, polluted. A city where old and new buildings stand side by side, fading nervously into the sky. Where the hotel we are given feels like secrets are contained in the small rooms, first hatched maybe in the roomy, airy bar and reception. Outside the air feels slightly dank, tight.

On my first night there I go to Guigsy's banquet room with Mikey. They tell me that pot is addictive. I don't believe them. 'When I'm on tour,' Guigsy explains, 'if I know it's not there, not going to be available at the next town or gig, I have to psych myself up. I have to spend the day as calm as I can and at night I have to go to bed early and try and ignore the sweating. If that doesn't happen I am up all night.'

'Why bother then? Knock it on the head.'

'Not that easy. See, when I don't have spliff there's something not right, like I'm a little off balance. Spark up and that's it. I connect with everything. Everything is sweet. If it's not, I get poorly. So much for it not being addictive.'

*

The phone rings early in the morning. It's Noel. Wants to go shopping. We meet in the lobby, Coyley as well. Noel tells us that the gig in Chile is under threat. Pinochet has just stepped down and no one knows what is going to happen next.

We find the main street, check the shops. Noel is rarely recognized. Which is all right by him. And me. It means you don't have to stop every two minutes and listlessly wait around while he signs paper, exchanges pleasantries.

Noel buys four pair of trainers. Wants to know why I don't get any. I don't tell him I'm a bit short on the cashola front. Believe me, it's a bit of a bastard shopping with a multi-millionaire when funds are low.

*

We stop off in a bar for a drink. Which becomes plural. Which becomes a night on the tiles. At some point we go back to the hotel. The promoter is waiting, wants us to go to another bar and watch football. We do so. Don't know why. Game is a blur.

On to another bar. Pool table. Beat Noel. Fifty quid a game, but he doesn't pay. I would have done. Which is probably why he's rich. And I'm not.

Sit with Coyley and enthuse about lovers, their healing power, how they make you better people. He loves Oasis, Coyley, would die for them. He says, 'No one in this band has ever let me down. Not once. And they never will.'

Where does it go from here? 'As far as I'm concerned the future of the band is all down to Liam. Noel will go on writing songs until they put the last screw in his coffin. You've heard his new material, tear-jerking stuff. He'll keep on giving Liam great songs to sing. It's how much he wants to sing them.'

That vital question: How much do you want it? It still echoes down the years.

*

And that night Noel said of Liam: 'I don't care how provoked he was, you don't go round leathering people. Simple as that. And what I'd like to know is, where the fuck was Terry? Fuck me,' he says breaking into a resigned grin, 'we should get a bodyguard for him.'

*

Bad head the next day and then off to Santiago. The flight is short and sweet. It's a funny thing to say but given the amount of flying on this tour, planes are like taxis for most of us. Only you don't have to hand over a tip at the end of the flight.

On the way to the hotel we pass through shanty towns, poverty. Kids in cheap clothes with big eyes stare impassively as we sweep by. Music can fight many things. But not poverty. Oasis are in town? Big deal for these children.

*

The hotel is large, expensive, big rooms. Young fans wait outside and scream when we pull up. Then as we walk to our rooms they crowd around a window. A lone security guard appears and chases their screams into the distance.

*

The gig is at the San Carlos de Apoquindo stadium. Capacity is 28,707. At least 30,000 people will witness the gig. The altitude is such that in the dressing room Steve Allen is showing the band how to use an oxygen mask. Just before Noel puts on his mask, he says, 'This is what I'm going to be like in 30 years' time, standing on a stage with an oxygen mask going, "This is an old song of ours, it's called, 'I Wish I'd Never Started Taking Drugs'".'

*

Liam's voice is croaky, but by the time they get to 'Champagne Supernova' he is in full flight. The gig itself is in such a great setting. Mountains loom in the distance, there are red scars on the darkening sky and the young crowd is so joyful, so open in their love for Oasis, that you can't help but love their passion, their life.

And when Noel Gallagher sits alone and sings 'Live Forever' on an acoustic guitar and the people who have suffered in ways we'll never know, sing the words back as if they were blowing him kisses, it really is one of those fantastic moments in your life, cherished forever.

*

The next morning I'm packing and the phone rings. It's Meg, looking for Noel. His phone is constantly engaged. Will I run down and tell him that she needs to talk to him? Sure thing. I catch the lift down, locate his room and knock on his door. Noel opens up. He looks absolutely wasted as if he has been howling at the moon all night. His eyes are gone, his balance spectacularly unsteady. 'Noel, Meg . . .' He raises a hand in the air. Leave it at that, he is saying. I understand. The poor fucker can't talk. Sure thing.

*

Back to noisy Buenos Aires and then dinner with Marcus. Mike Rowe and Strangeboy are also present. Everything is going well until the Liam incident in Australia is raised. 'To be honest, I fear like fuck for him,' Marcus said. And he said it with such feeling that we all went quiet, looked at the plates in front of us.

It really was an uncomfortable moment, to feel the manager's worry.

*

When we get back to the hotel, Noel excitedly calls me over. 'He's here.'

'You're joking.'

'I'm fucking not. He's upstairs. We saw him coming in with his entourage, so one of the chaps went over and told him we were in the hotel. He's having something to eat and then he's coming down in a minute to meet us and do a photograph. Stick around.'

'Well, I'm not going anywhere, am I? Fucking hell, I can't believe it.'

Then the word came down. He would only meet Noel and Liam. That was it. They were to go up to the suite. No others would be allowed in. Noel looked at me like, What the fuck can I do? I know you should meet him as much as

I should but . . . It's OK, boss. I'm sure he'll come to the gig. It's cool. At some point in our stay, I am absolutely certain I will get to shake the hand of Diego Armando Maradona, the world's greatest footballer.

*

The first thing they noticed was how many women were in the room. Plenty. Then they were introduced. He extravagantly kissed Noel's big crucifix and his ring. Then Diego stood in the corner of the room and played tricks, looking to impress them. Like a child would. He juggled an orange with both feet. He placed a small opened bottle of Evian water on his forehead and didn't spill a drop. Then he posed for a photograph with the boys and as the camera clicked, he whispered to Liam, 'The girls, you don't take them with you, OK?' The Gallagher brothers laughed. Already they liked him.

Then Liam said, 'You, world's greatest player.' He didn't want to use the past tense and insult him. This was Diego Armando Maradona and you showed him maximum respect. 'I still am,' Maradona simply replied.

*

In the bar downstairs I waited and when Noel walked back in he was so flushed, so excited, that it was contagious. This was a moment in his life. You don't get that many. Cheer them when you do. We went to my room to celebrate. Noel told me, 'Don't worry, man. He says he's definitely coming to the gig and then he's coming here on Wednesday to see us off.'

*

Noel sat watching football. We – Phil, Liam, Terry, Steve and others – chatted, drank beer in my small room. But things were brewing. Noel kept glancing at Liam. Finally, he had to let it out.

Noel: I'm sorry but it's wrong to leather a fan.

Liam: He wasn't a fan. Fuck he was. I was in the right and if I have to go down for it then I'll do it because I was right.

Noel: Oh, you were right, whacking someone? That's right, is it?

Liam: Yes, because he asked for it. And all I want is a fair trial and I don't think I am going to get it.

Noel: So you're going to carry on whacking people?

Liam: No, I'll never do it again. I've learnt the hard way from this one.

Noel: So you're saying you'll never do it again?

Liam: No I won't. But I tell you what. That fucking geezer deserved it.

*

Later on:

Liam: You don't write for money. You write because you have to. You'll still be writing at 40. Fucking right you will.

Noel: Oh, you know that, do you? Know that for sure.

Liam: Yeah, I do.

Noel: Well, let me tell you, there is no way whatsoever I will be on a stage at 40 years old going, 'You got to roll with it . . .' No fucking way, man.

Liam: Nor will I, but we ain't talking about that.

Noel: What we talking about then?

Liam: Songwriting.

Noel: And you know about that, do you?

Liam: No, dickhead. We're talking about your song-writing and the fact that you'll be hammering away at it in the future.

Noel: I'll tell you what I'm going to do. What I'm going to do is make enough money so that I – we – never have to work again. Do you know what I'm going to do then? I'm going to get fat. I'm going to sit at home and watch TV and get enormous.

Liam: Yeah, but you'll still be writing songs.

Noel: Will I? How do you know?

Liam: I just do.

Noel: How?

Liam (leaning forward): Because I'm your brother.

*

They left round about six a.m., I guess. I dreamt of Noel holding his crucifix and ring up to me and saying, 'I've done it all, biggest gig, biggest album, but this beats it all. He kissed my ring. He kissed my ring.'

*

Sony had challenged the band to a football match. None of them showed, so me and the road crew hopped into the van and were taken to an indoor stadium. 'Are some of the lifts out?' I asked Roger, Guigsy's man, as we negotiated the crowded streets. 'I waited about ten minutes for one,' I explained, 'and when it came it was rammed. Had to walk 12 floors down.'

'Where the fuck have you been all day, Mr On The Spot Writer?'

'Sleeping.'

'That explains it.'

Here's the gist of it all. After leaving my room Liam had opted to keep going, drank Jack and coke all day. Meanwhile fans had now gathered outside the hotel. Some of them had slept the night on the steps. The hotel management then suggested opening up a room where Noel could meet them, sign some autographs. Then they could go home and the hotel could stop worrying if one of them died in the cold and on their premises. Fine.

Noel, who had slept, met up with Terry and they waited by the lifts. Enter Liam. Off his head. Where you going? Noel explains and of course Liam wants to come along. Feels left out. An argument ensues. Noel tells him to fuck off and get. some sleep.

Terry says it too. But leaves out the fuck-off bit. Doesn't matter. Right now it's all red rag to Gallagher Junior. Liam explodes.

You're washed up, he tells his brother. Finished. Gone. Your songs are shit. Everyone knows it but I'm the only one who will fucking tell you. As for you, Terry, fuck you, you're sacked.

Then he goes into an empty lift and he kicks and punches and he kicks again until there is glass everywhere and the buttons don't work and suddenly, brutally, one of the lifts is damaged beyond belief.

*

For the third time in six months a hotel manager sees no option in front of him except to say, leave. Go now. It's not as though they were particularly happy about our stay anyway, given their knowledge of events in Australia and elsewhere. When we arrived, they began closing the bar at 11, posting a couple more security guards in reception. Now there was a smashed lift and over a thousand pissed-off guests to deal with. This they really can do without.

So here we go again. Oasis, pack your bags. Now. Go. Don't Be Here Now. Be gone now. Now there's a real problem because every other hotel in town is full. There is literally nowhere for us to go. Finally, for the third time in six months, a hotel manager has to relent and let us stay. If our cards had been marked before they were definitely stamped 'undesirable' now.

But far worse than that, and of real concern, was that it really felt like Liam was spiralling so far out of control that soon nobody – and I mean nobody – would be able to reach him. His behaviour was starting to touch upon the frightening. He must have felt it as well.

*

The next day at the gig Liam, shaved, bright-eyed and quiet, actually turned up for the soundcheck. He sang with vigour and energy while an excited queue which stretched right round the Luna Park auditorium strained to hear every syllable.

At the gig itself, Noel played 'Live Forever' on acoustic guitar and again the crowd sang back the words and again I felt the power.

After the show three of the band quickly took off, while Liam and Bonehead chatted amicably to the young fans who crowded into the small dressing room. Some of the keener fans followed us back to the hotel for a drink. A pointless exercise. As soon as we walked in the hotel, staff swung into a quasi-military operation. Out of nowhere, heavy-set guys with shades and walkie-talkies appeared. Some stationed themselves by the newly repaired lifts, others by reception. The shutters on the bar came slamming down. Early night then.

*

Buenos Aires was doing everyone's head in. Everything – the hotel, the traffic, the weather – was so oppressive. A phone call home cost you the earth and the air outside felt poisoned. The only highlights were the young faces of the fans either outside the hotel or at the gig and those great moments in the set where Oasis hit such a stride that the music blew away your every complaint.

On top of that, he lied. Diego Armando Maradona never showed for any of the gigs. Or came to the hotel to say goodbye. I wiped away my regret and flew down to Rio.

*

Out in the sun, by the pool, watching two working girls in bikinis go to work on a young American. Bonehead, Whitey, Liam and Guigs order breakfast. Noel never comes out in the sun. He should have done. After Buenos Aires, these two hours we have lolling around the pool are the most relaxing that I can remember in a long time.

The famed Copacabana beach is 20 yards away, but we have been warned not to swim in the sea. We have also been warned not to leave the hotel. If we do then we must take someone with us. Never ever, they tell us, travel alone. And if you ignore this advice, then quite frankly you deserve to have your kidneys cut out and sold abroad. Still, as I tell Noel, he needn't worry too much about losing his kidneys. 'State of yours, they'll probably pay you to take them back.'

*

The translator in the van points to a cluster of houses that climb up a hill. 'That's where the drug barons live,' he informs us. 'The police daren't go near there.'

'Why not?' Strangeboy asks.

'Because the drug people are better armed than them.'

*

Whatever troubles hang over Oasis, these South American shows are blowing them away with a vengeance. The crowd's reaction is so intoxicating, so exciting to experience, that it's genuinely creating a new and far more positive energy which galvanizes everyone involved. After Australia, funky days are here again.

Away from the numbers and the pressure and the endless sniping and the talking and the arguing and the press and all the things that get in the way of the communication, Oasis are the recipients of huge and true love. It reminds them that in the scheme of things, they ain't doing too bad.

*

On the way to Sao Paulo, Noel turned to Paolo and said, 'Did you see MTV last night? I am such a dithering idiot sometimes. This guy's asking me all these questions and I'm standing there going, Well, yeah, maybe, I mean . . . So I'm sitting there watching all this and I'm really getting annoyed with myself. I'm shouting at the TV, Go on, say something, you dick. I mean, no wonder Meg won't phone me. Where are you? Well, I think I'm in my room but then again I might not be . . .'

Humour regained.

*

Halfway through the show at the Polo de Arte e Cultura do Anhembi stadium, where at least 15,000 Brazilians are now flicking their lighters at the band and singing 'Wonderwall' after giving Oasis a standing ovation for their version of 'Stand By Me' (and that's the third song in), Marcus turns to me and says, 'Steve Sutherland, the *NME* editor, was right. This band is finished.' And then he laughs his tits off.

The next day Bonehead lashed out. It was the anniversary of his mother's death and he had been up all night drinking. Now, in the afternoon that we are due to book out and fly to Mexico, he sits with Whitey in the bar of this huge Maksoud Plaza hotel in Sao Paulo and urges the bar band to perform, of all things, 'Happy Mother's Day'. 'Come on, play me that song,' he urges, but thankfully the band, they don't understand English.

Whitey is doing his best to keep Bonehead on an even keel but it's an impossible task. Tears are now starting to stream down the guitarist's face, his voice is cracking fast. 'I need some red wine, Whitey,' he tells his friend, 'or someone is going to get it.'

I tell Whitey, 'You stay there, I'll get it', then hurriedly walk to the bar, but before I can get there I hear shouting. I turn and see Bonehead stalking the hotel foyer, telling everyone – guests, security guards, hotel employees – that he's ready to do them. Anyone. Come on! Who wants it?

Suddenly Danny appears and gently takes Bonehead and expertly guides him to the lift. Whitey watches Bonehead ascend in the glass lift to his room. The drummer's face is filled with concern. Since his recruitment to the band, Bonehead and he have become firm friends. Whitey puts down his glass. 'I better go up and sort him out,' he gently says.

*

At the airport, the Mexico plane is delayed. We procure drinks, Noel sets up his CD player and we sit around, talking, examining. Noel's musical selection includes The Left Banke (a gift from a sussed fan), The Creation. Coyley digs these old tunes, thinks modern music has lost it. 'You know when you wake up in the morning and you know you've had a good night because there are crusty bits around your eyes and your mouth and you look at them and know you've had a top time? Well, that's what music needs now, big fucking crusty bits!'

'Too fucking right,' Noel shouts. He flicks out Neil Young's music for the Johnny Depp film *Dead Man*. For Noel, this is Depp's acting at its finest, oblique but powerful. And for Coyley, Neil Young is the Manchester United of the music world.

'Best ever,' Coyley says of Young. 'Better than The Beatles by a mile. Never wrote a pop song in his life.'

'What did you fucking say?'

Guess who?

Liam looms over us. He was walking by when he heard that last statement. Coyley repeats it to him. Neil Young over The Beatles, each and every way.

'Rubbish,' sneers Liam.

'Why?' Coyley challenges.

'Because he's not the King. You know who the King is.'

'Who's that then?'

'John Lennon. And anyway Neil Young can't be King because he's not dead, and to be King you must be dead. Simple.'

Liam walks away and, in his best croaking voice, Noel says, 'Get thee behind me, Satan.'

*

Two shows, one long flight, that's it. Finito.

Our last hotel is a beauty. All the rooms, these spacious rooms, look out onto a colourful, peaceful garden. We are protected from the hustle of the city, stuck away in comfort. What's more, this joint is owned by the Four Seasons chain. I don't know whose weaving the magic but The Extinguisher in Milan Incident seems to have been quietly forgotten.

I shower, eat, watch David Byrne make a complete prat of himself on TV and then hop into a van with Noel, Rob, Strangeboy and Phil, and journey to the outskirts of Mexico City.

For Noel this is a pilgrimage, the journey he has been waiting all his life to make, to take the road that leads to the pyramids. He was brought up a Catholic, but the cosmic tapestry that weaves together the building of pyramids with, alien existence, exerts a far stronger influence on his beliefs, his spirituality.

These pyramids, built in Teotihuacan, represent to Noel real proof that we are part of a master plan that is not only breathtaking in its scale but has been deliberately hidden from us for centuries. Now he will get a glimpse of its scale and reaffirm his beliefs.

The girl who works for the promoter has laid on a guide. He keeps calling us Big Boys. 'Over here, Big Boy,' he cheerfully shouts. He is Mexican Indian. He tells us, much to our regret, that just days before, Indians from all over the world had gathered here for their spring solstice, celebrated the realignment of the stars for three days.

'Imagine that,' Noel said deliciously, 'three days of looking at the stars and munching on peyote.'

'Sounds like the tour,' jokes Strangeboy.

There are two pyramids to visit, one dedicated to the Sun, the other to the Moon. We visit the Sun pyramid first, climb about 250 steep steps to reach its summit. It is three in the afternoon. Hot and dusty, I walk behind Noel.

As we grimly make our ascent, a young American boy passes us on the way down. The expression on his face as Noel passes him, huffing and sweating, and he gradually recognizes the musician, is absolutely priceless. Check it from his point of view. Here he is on holiday in Mexico, walking down a pyramid and minding his own business and who should walk past him? Only his favourite musician. Noel is concentrating too hard on reaching the top to notice.

At the pyramid's summit we gather our breath, massage aching legs. Then the guide leads us into some basic Indian ceremonies. We throw brightly coloured pebbles into the air as an offering to the Gods and feel like we're standing on the top of the world, able to touch Heaven.

The view is absolutely breathtaking. You can see for miles and miles, can't help but admire the green flat-lands that stretch into the so distant horizon. A good place to worship.

About halfway down, Noel is approached by the young American, who has gathered together his equally amazed friends. Noel happily signs autographs, poses for pictures. Then they go home and boast for weeks about grabbing Noel Gallagher's autograph. Halfway up a pyramid.

The guide takes us to other parts of the site, explains how the pyramids here are built to the same scale as those in Egypt, even though there was absolutely no communication between the cultures. He tells us that to date 11,000 pyramids have been discovered in Mexico and he makes a point of explaining their early heating systems. This is a proud Indian. Rightly so.

We move on to the Moon pyramid. It's a shorter climb, some 165 steps. Again the view is magnificent, the moment heightened by the knowledge of us treading ancient hallowed ground.

Noel says little throughout the journey. He has studied these pyramids, this culture. He simply nods at the facts the guide tells us, knows most of them anyway. Guides being guides, he has, of course, a friend who runs a shop that we just have to visit. We buy small souvenirs, Noel nearly buys the shop.

We wander outside into the heat and the guide points out his favourite animal, a donkey that drinks from any bottle you place in front of him. 'Should take him on the road,' Noel says, 'keep Liam company in the bar after we've all pissed off.'

Exhausted now by the heat, the walking, we clamber back into the van. Noel has a press conference at the hotel in an hour's time. 'This book you're doing,' Noel says wearily from the back of his seat, 'I don't give a shit what you write but you put in there that today was no joke for me. Today I made a pilgrimage. I have been waiting years for today. Absolute fucking years. You put that in.'

So I did.

*

At these press conferences, Noel always looked for the smart-arse reply. No way was he going to get deep. That was hard enough in a one-on-one situation. No way would it happen in a room with 300 writers present. Instead, he put on his arrogant head. Three answers illustrate the point.

How has success changed you?

'I suppose it's made me a bit more spiritual . . . About the amount of money we've got in the bank!'

Has technology changed music?

'I don't think technology has affected music. There's either good music or bad music. And the good music is generally written by me.'

Are you better than God? You certainly act it.

'Um, well, eh . . . What was the last good tune He wrote?'

*

On Wednesday 25 March 1998, Coyley married his girl Ruth Farrell. They had been seeing each other for years. Noel was best man. A mariachi band serenaded them. Champagne was drunk, people hugged, the sun shone and there were smiles everywhere. The girls looked pretty, the boys smart. It was a great ending to the tour, a real feeling of new beginnings for everyone present.

*

And at the last gig of the Be Here Now tour Noel's amp burst into flames. For absolutely no reason whatsoever.

Jason, Noel's roadie, was the first to spot it. He simply ran on stage and pulled Noel away. Noel looked at him like he was mad and then he saw the fire behind him. I thought someone had thrown a firecracker.

Then I looked up and there were Liam and Noel standing at the front of the stage, arms round each other and jumping up and down. Just like they did a million years ago on that night in the studio when *Be Here Now* was unveiled.

*

Liam was buzzing. He couldn't wait for Oasis's future to begin. 'It's like when you wake up and have a full breakfast,' he enthused, cooling down in the dressing room. 'I'm just mopping up the egg with my fried bread. I haven't chosen my clobber for the day yet. I haven't read the papers. I haven't even put *Richard and Judy* on. I'm just dipping my bread into my egg. Imagine what happens when I leave the house. Imagine what happens then. And that's us, Oasis, man. We're not even out of our pyjamas.' And he flicked and clicked his fingers, victorious.

*

The end-of-tour party at the hotel was a bore and a washout. No music could be played, conversation was kept at a minimum level. There were no outbreaks of drunken behaviour, no shouting, screaming and fighting between anyone present. We sat around large tables covered in white cloth and waited for things to happen. And they never did.

It was a sedate ending to a six-month tour that had taken Oasis all around the world, where they had touched the lives of a million people and had their lives touched too, changed them slightly.

They would take a lot of time off now. A lot of time. And then they would return. For in the last six months they had discovered that they were still important to people, that their music had a currency that could not be obliterated. They had found their meaning, their direction, and they now saw new goals for them to achieve. This game was far from over. Oasis was all and The Sons of the Stage would have to wait.

Once again they had nearly broken themselves in two, but again they had saved themselves because above all else this band were fighters and other options were just far too easy.

And as I sat at a table with Noel and a host of Mexican fans and surveyed all the people who had been my family for the past six months. I realized that tomorrow they would be gone. Different paths, different lives. No phone calls to the room, no room service, no gigs, soundchecks, the endless waiting around in large dressing rooms. No struggling to find conversation or watching egos struggle, no banter, no more lightweights or good drinks.

Just home and a gradual easing out of the bubble. I knew now what life would be like for me in the next month. It would be exactly what I and all of us had been trying to escape, probably all our lives. It was the real world and it was waiting patiently for all of us at nine the next day. At Heathrow Airport. Terminal one, I do believe.

But in these last few hours I would ignore it. I wouldn't be up or down. I would just be content to be here now.

THE EPILOGUE

AND he did: close Oasis down. After the last show there were discreet murmurs of the band heading straight into the studio to work on new material. Such talk reflected the high levels of playing that extensive touring had engendered between all five members. It was not to be.

Noel Gallagher kept to his word and decided to lay low for a while.

Before entering a period of rest, Noel's first move was to record his instrumental composition 'Teotihaucan' for the *X Files* film. It was his first solo effort, using samples and a recurring piano riff to create effective, brooding music. At the time he called it 'the best thing I've ever done'.

*

In the summer, after avidly watching the World Cup, Noel began writing a new batch of songs. They had titles such as 'Gas Panic,' 'Cigarettes In Hell' and 'Revolution Song'.

Every so often, he, along with allies such as Coyley or Strangeboy, would enter a studio and record his work to date. Noel, as far as I could hear, had chosen not to rely on the songs he already had but to create entirely new music.

The other members, in turn, had also been productive.

Guigsy set up his own home studio and began creating dub-influenced music.

*

Liam and Bonehead also wrote songs, Liam in particular finishing off a maddeningly catchy tune called 'Little James', which he would sing 200 times to anyone who would sit near him. Even Alan White, when spotted once in public, talked of 'a symphony in my head I'd like to get down'.

All of them had invested in home studios. Touring, it seemed, had activated all their creative buttons.

*

When he wasn't writing or recording, Noel either partied, holidayed or opted to work with other artists. In the summer of 1998 he made surprise solo support appearances on Paul Weller's tour, playing acoustic versions of songs such as 'Wonderwall' and 'Talk Tonight'. He co-wrote a song with The Chemical Brothers and later played a dockers' benefit in London which ended with Noel and Steve Cradock of Ocean Colour Scene joining Pete Townshend of The Who to thrash their way through his song 'Magic Bus'. Of his contemporaries, Noel became a huge admirer of The Beta Band, a couple of his demos making overt nods towards their heavy percussion style.

*

In October 1998 Oasis briefly returned to the spotlight with the release of their b-side album, *The Masterplan*. They conducted little promotion on its behalf – a couple of music-press interviews, no radio or TV – but their immense popularity was reflected in its buoyant sales. Within two weeks it had sold 300,000 copies in the UK alone. The album also garnered huge critical praise from all media. Some writers even dubbed it the best-ever Oasis album.

Noel had a good Christmas.

By March 1999 he had two things on his mind. First there was the impending court case with the band's former drummer, Tony McCarroll. This was a worrying affair. Although on the surface McCarroll's claim to some £18 million of Oasis money seemed highly unlikely to succeed, the final decision on the matter would rest with just one judge. Given that most judges' grip on the workings of a pop group remain somewhat tenuous, the case represented a gamble.

Happily, on the first day of the trial, McCarroll accepted a settlement and signed away all his rights to Oasis material past and future.

Noel now pulled the band together for two weeks of rehearsals in Bermondsey's Music Bank rehearsal studios. By now he had 23 songs that he considered strong enough for the album.

The group also attended a party to mark the opening of designer Tommy Hilfiger's West End shop. Liam harangued the designer for working with The Rolling Stones, and Bonehead, on leaving the party, insulted a bouncer and then a passing policeman. He was arrested and spent a night in the cells, although he did not drop his trousers at the waiting press pack.

On 27 March, Oasis flew to France to record their fourth album. Noel's initial idea of having a multitude of producers work on the material had now been shelved. He had opted instead to use Spike Dent, whose work he knew from U2's *Achtung Baby* album. It was sometime later that Noel discovered his subsequent work with The Spice Girls.

At time of writing, Noel had two titles for the album under consideration, one of which was 'Where Did It All Go Wrong?' It is highly unlikely that this will be used.

THE END